W9-CPP-984

*Girl in Pink*                    Portland Museum of Art

www.meyersphoto.com

Although Gilchrist did not use symbolism in his work, the large, stunningly beautiful, life-sized oil called *Girl in Pink* clearly introduces an element of mystery and may even have ventured into the symbolic. Look for a moment at the photograph of this painting and see whether anything is slightly amiss in the sitter's eyes.

The woman looks to our right and has no easily defined expression on her face, at least not on the side we are allowed to see. In the mirror, however, her reflection shows a woman whose eyes are closed, or so nearly closed that we see only her eyelid. Her head is angled in a slightly different direction, too, so that no one could possibly take the reflection to be a simply photographic one. Once we acknowledge this deliberate inconsistency, it becomes clear that Gilchrist did not intend this to be an ordinary painting. If we search the work of the painters he admired, such as Whistler, who did a very similar painting called *Symphony in White, #2: The Little White Girl*, the mystery remains, because in Whistler's work the eyes are correctly reflected. The similarity lies only in the use of the mirror and the profile view, not in the substance.

Gilchrist was thirty-one when he completed this masterpiece, the father of three small children and already a painter of considerable stature. Behind his often charming personality, however, lay one overriding anxiety, from which, as the burdens on him grew, there came from time to time a nightmarish desperation to achieve all he possibly could while he still had the strength. His heart disease, while not disabling until his late forties, was nonetheless not curable, and while his spirit naturally sought release, his reason told him clearly that in the end the disease would kill him.

It makes sense to say that at some point this primary struggle in his life would work its way into his painting, however subtly. What is remarkable is that he managed to insert the enigma of the eyes so quietly and naturally that for years it passed unnoticed. The painting shows the serene, sensual beauty of a young woman who is gorgeously clothed and perfectly posed, a woman with a face as lovely and unreadable as Mona Lisa's. Behind her, hovering ghostlike in the darkly painted mirror, lies the sure sign of tragedy, the hardship and heartbreak of ephemeral beauty. Here, in contrast to the spectacular perfection of his subject, is the ineffable sadness of age and the stark inevitability of death.

In a very real sense Gilchrist himself was the male version of this wonderfully feminine creation, for he, too, was fatally flawed, and though he forced himself to keep a brave and even serene exterior, he knew only too well that his days would not be numerous enough to encompass all he wanted to do. The *Girl in Pink* may look like just another beautiful portrait, but if so it is also the most personal, and the most powerful, painting Gilchrist ever did.

# Affectionately, Wallace

The Life and Work of

## W. W. GILCHRIST

ROBERT GRIFFIN

www.meyersphoto.com

*Nelly at Age 5*

www.meyersphoto.com

*Parisian Bonnet*

www.meyersphoto.com

*Girl on Seacoast*

# DEDICATION

*Bill at Sunset*

On March 22, 1995, Bill Gilchrist, my mother's younger brother, the artist's only son, and my only living link with W. Wallace Gilchrist, Jr., passed away in Freeport, Maine, after a long and gallant struggle with Parkinson's disease. In countless chats with Bill during his last years, he told me things about his father that gave spirit and meaning to the dry facts I knew already. During these long talks, Bill and I, uncle and nephew, easily bridged the twenty-six years separating us and became friends. His twinkling good humor, sharp mind, and powerful desire to live his life to the hilt despite the ravages of Parkinson's, were an inspiration to all the nurses, doctors, and family members who waited on him.

During these slowly declining years of his life, I began to see in him the spirit of his father. Through our talks I felt I was hearing the voices of two men and learning the maps of their emotional lives, their dreams and sufferings and their passions and fears. I saw the courage of both men to keep struggling for life. I saw their boundless capacity for happiness, joy, and love.

Never while I sat with him did he speak a word of complaint. He was not bitter about the insidious disease that was quietly robbing him of life. Instead, he told me that old age was a challenge and gamely set himself the task of writing his autobiography, a long and painstaking process performed by finger muscles barely able to move a pencil. When I began typing it for him, he was very grateful, and it was typical of his unselfishness that when he realized I was too busy to continue, he spent the money to hire a professional typist. Like his father, Bill never had a lot of money and often suffered for the lack of it; yet such was his popularity that he seldom lacked the essentials, and his five children would drop everything to rush to his side from all over the country if he suddenly worsened, as happened several times.

More than anyone else, it was Bill who gave this chronicle life, who told me the stories, who showed me all the lovely old homes his family occupied in Brunswick and Portland, and who was so obviously the spiritual descendant of the artist. Although it is sad that he died before he could hold this book in his hands, I know from what he once told me that he was ready to die, that his soul was aching to take flight from the wreck his poor body had become. And so, Bill, I say a farewell to you on your last journey, hoping you will again see your father and mother and sisters in a better place than this battered world. I dedicate these pages to you and all your family and hope they will reveal to their readers just what sort of man Wallace Gilchrist really was.

www.meyersphoto.com

Wally Books
Bridgton, Maine
2001

Copies of this book can be ordered from Wally Books, RR2, Box 581,
Bridgton, ME 04009, for $29.95 plus $3.05 shipping and handling.
Maine residents add sales tax. Please allow three weeks for delivery.

COVER
*Family Circle* by W. W. Gilchrist, photograph by Bernard C. Meyers

ACKNOWLEDGMENTS
I would like to thank the following people for the help and encouragement
they have offered throughout the duration of this project: Kathleen Kenny,
Barbara Olmstead, Phil Beam, Buddy Gilchrist, Alan Burbank, George
deSchweinitz, Bill Gilchrist, John Lorence, Bill Imes, Jim Storer, Pat Gerber,
Scot Dimond, Chris Crosman, and the people at the Curtis Memorial
Library in Brunswick.

SOURCES
The vast majority of the information contained in these pages comes from a
family scrapbook, from letters found among family members, and from old
issues of the *Brunswick Record*. All of the family documents have been
donated to Special Collections at the Bowdoin College Library in Brunswick,
Maine. The library also has back issues of the *Record* on microfilm.

PRINTED BY
J. S. McCarthy / Letter Systems, Augusta, Maine

PUBLISHED BY
Wally Books, Bridgton, Maine

DESIGN BY
Mahan Graphics, Bath, Maine

PHOTOGRAPHY BY
Bernard C. Meyers (where noted)

EDITED BY
Susan L. Ransom, Portland, Maine

INDEXER
Emma Stephenson

Library of Congress Control Number: 2001089568

ISBN: 0-9712405-0-7

© copyright 2001 by Frederick R. Griffin

All rights reserved
No part of this publication may be reproduced or transmitted in any form or
by any means, electronic or mechanical, including photocopy, recording, or
any information storage and retrieval system, without permission in writing
from the publisher.

INTRODUCTION

LIST OF ILLUSTRATIONS

www.meyersphoto.com

*Reading by Lamplight*

## INTRODUCTION

As a small boy, I was curious about the man in the photograph on my mother's dresser. He was your grandfather, she said, a painter. You mean Grandma's husband, I asked. Yes, she said, but he died before you were born; he was forty-seven years old when he died. Mommy, what happens to us if you die young like your father? You needn't worry about that because the doctors know a lot more now, she said.

Still, I worried, and from that moment on, during all my years growing up, getting married, raising two daughters, going through two careers, getting divorced, and finally becoming a grandfather myself, the seed of a book was growing inside. It was growing so quietly that until the day I said to my second wife, "I want to do my grandfather's life," I had no idea it was there.

I went to the local library and looked up William Wallace Gilchrist, Jr., and almost gave up then because there was almost nothing written about him. Yet the need to create something beautiful and memorable about this man simply would not release me. I spoke to his other grandchildren, and my cousin Alan Burbank out in California sent me a beautiful book on an exhibition of American Impressionist paintings held in 1980 at the Henry Art Gallery of the University of Washington in Seattle.

I read this book cover to cover, and I was so captivated by the paintings that I moved on to other books on the American painters of the period. Then I got my first real break. Alan sent me a packet of letters he had found, left to him by his mother, my Aunt Nelly. These letters were written by the young painter to his father during his first trip to Europe between September 1900 and April 1901. In their revelation of feelings and attitudes of a young, freshly educated painter, they are priceless.

In 1990, my uncle, the artist's son, was retired and living in the old farmhouse in Cundy's Harbor, Maine. He was intensely interested in my project, and despite the insidious invasion of Parkinson's disease, he offered help at every turn. He loaned me a book on his grandfather, the Philadelphia musician, by Martha Furman Schliemann. When I went to see her, I made the second great discovery of this odyssey: my mother had loaned her the family scrapbook kept by the artist's older sister, Anna. After carefully checking me over, Mrs. Schliemann graciously returned the scrapbook to the family.

*Lady Lynx*

Also in 1990, my move from White Plains, New York, to Brunswick, Maine, led me to a third discovery: the old *Brunswick Record,* on microfilm in the Bowdoin College Library. This weekly newspaper is a fascinating source of information on life in early twentieth-century Maine, and so personal and thorough was the coverage that I found enough material for a whole chapter on the Gilchrists.

However, even with the scrapbook, the letters, the newspaper stories, and the personal recollections of the artist's son, the most vital thing was still missing: the paintings. Once again, my California cousin came to the rescue, recalling that his father had had the foresight to engage a Portland photographer named Bernie Meyers to photograph all the paintings in the highly successful Gilchrist exhibition at the Barridoff Galleries in the summer of 1984.

Another windfall came much later in the project, when I learned about a large number of watercolors, unframed, untitled, and unknown to most of the art world. It was almost as if Gilchrist had decided to leave them for his own family rather than take the trouble to sell them. It was my good fortune to be given the chance to use them in the book.

*The Locket*

Although his sister did keep a list of some of his paintings, and I have compiled lists from documented exhibitions (see List of Exhibitions), Gilchrist himself was not a careful keeper of records. I can only assume, therefore, that today there are dozens of Gilchrist portraits of which I have never heard, still gracing the living rooms and dens and dining rooms of the descendants of the original sitters, now long since gone to their graves.

# LIST OF PAINTINGS

Two letters written to the artist's sister, Anna, go into some detail on the first W. W. Gilchrist to set foot upon North American shores. One of these letters speaks of two Gilchrist brothers, supporters of Prince Charlie, who were forced to "leave Scotland in a hurry or lose their heads." The other letter speaks of a Gilchrist who "ran away with a daughter of the Argyles," an act that led to the expulsion of his entire clan from Scotland and their hurried relocation to northern Ireland. According to the first story, the two brothers arrived in North America and split up, never to see each other again. One settled near Montreal in Trois Rivieres (Three Rivers), Quebec; the other found green pastures in St. George, near Tenants Harbor, Maine.

More than a century later, Helen Gilchrist, a descendant of the Tenants Harbor brother, corresponded with Wallace's sister Anna, a descendant of the Trois Rivieres Gilchrist. Helen and Anna evidently knew each other well, Helen signing her letter with love. They also shared a fascination for the Gilchrist family's origins. In a letter dated September 8, 1950, when Anna was in her eightieth year, Helen writes that her branch of the family had once invited her to a family reunion held in Maine every August. "There I met a James Gilchrist," she writes, "who had all the records. Reda and I both went and were surprised at the many faces that were true Gilchrist—blue eyes, pink cheeks, and golden hair. The old house was still standing (built in 1700s) when I first came but has since gone."

The Canadian Gilchrist may or may not have been the same man who involved himself recklessly with a daughter of the Argyles, but he definitely had an eye for the ladies. He met Janet Grant, daughter of James Grant, a prosperous man who was soon thereafter most unhappily surprised to learn that his daughter was in a family way thanks to the first W. W. Gilchrist. The two young lovers and prospective parents, living in the blind bliss of their romance, were harshly disillusioned when Mr. Grant refused to take them under his roof. In fact so flatly and thoroughly did he refuse that William hastily chose to leave the area.

Not long thereafter, the new grandfather relented and took back his daughter so that she could raise her son, also named W. W. Gilchrist, in a respectable and secure home. It was this little boy, born in 1818, who eventually married into the Cox family and fathered the famous Philadelphia musician.

While Janet Grant Gilchrist's son William was growing up in Montreal, a well-known New York builder named Jacob Cox was hired to do the roofing for the city's great Cathedral of Notre Dame. Jacob arrived in Montreal with his daughter, Anna Redelia, age seven, and promptly placed her schooling in the hands of the Convent of the Grey Nuns directly under the eaves of the enormous cathedral. For the next seven years, Anna lived next door to Janet Grant Gilchrist and her son. The two families soon became such good friends that when the two Gilchrists decided to move to New York City, they moved right in with the Coxes.

The childhood friendship of Anna and William culminated in their marriage, and one of the fruits of this marriage, arriving on January 8, 1846, was a third W. W. Gilchrist, the one who in 1855 moved from Jersey City down to Philadelphia and, after serving briefly with the Union army, began his illustrious career in music.

www.meyersphoto.com

*W. W. Gilchrist, Sr.*

On May 19, 1861, when young Willy was fifteen years old, he received a letter from his Uncle Charlie (Charles Cox) in New York telling him all the war talk brought on by the attack on Fort Sumter. Uncle Charlie also invited Willy to the July 4th celebrations in New York that summer. Two years later, in January of 1863, Willy turned seventeen, and though he was below draft age, the patriotic fever of the day induced him to enlist with his older brother James, a physician.

Willy's mother, Anna Redelia Cox Gilchrist, wrote several letters to her two sons congratulating them on their patriotism and urging them to stay warm, keep dry, and watch what they ate. Willy served as a drummer boy and, fortunately for the music world, never saw combat. In July his mother, perhaps moved by the carnage at Gettysburg, wrote again and urged him not to stay longer than three months. When Willy wrote back complaining of ill health, Anna Redelia at once prevailed upon her husband to write to a Colonel Day begging for his early discharge. There is no evidence in the letters that he was released early, but when he did finally come home, he brought with him his little drum, which his son the artist kept in his studio at Roadside.

Only some unpleasant memories of sore feet and indigestible green apples marred the experience. In that grim moment of American history fortune smiled upon the Gilchrists; the horrible meat grinder of our nation's worst war did not number W. W. Gilchrist among the 600,000 men it killed. Instead it allowed him to go on to musical distinction and to produce in his son a marvelous painter.

After Willy's return, his mother actively promoted the union of her son and Susan Beaman, whom she described as one of "the best and prettiest and most patriotic of girls." Willy, however, was only seventeen and wisely decided to begin his studies before embarking on married life. The next two years are a blank, but in 1865 he began three years of lessons under Hugh Clarke at the University of Pennsylvania. Five years later, on June 8, 1870, he married Susie, and on May 29 of the following year Anna Redelia, the artist's only sister, was born. The young couple lived briefly in Cincinnati but returned to Philadelphia to raise Anna and their three sons, Charlie, Wallace, and Teddy. By 1885, the year of Teddy's birth, the Gilchrist family, now six strong, was living on Wayne Avenue in Mt. Airy, just north of the Philadelphia city limits.

According to a tenant interviewed in 1988, the house at 5914 Wayne Avenue was built by a wealthy man named Houston with money made as a shareholder or executive of the Pennsylvania Railroad. It is set back about thirty feet from the sidewalk, rises three stories, and attaches to another house, its twin, at 5912 Wayne Avenue. When the Gilchrists lived there, the two units were undivided and made a handsome and spacious dwelling for a family of six.

*Self-portrait*

The strip between the avenue and the house was grassy, planted with shrubbery, and well-shaded a century or so after the Gilchrists' residence there. Inside the house the ceilings are high, the walls are of plaster, and it is cool on a hot day in the summer. The staircases have old banisters with beautifully carved supports, and the visitor is pleasantly surprised to discover skylights on the third floor, which can be opened as an exhaust for the fierce heat of a Philadelphia summer.

Each floor has two rooms, front and rear. One can imagine that when the Gilchrists lived there, before the house was bisected, there was adequate room for all their sleeping, eating, and living requirements. The house had no less than five fireplaces and mantelpieces of distinction. The hardwood floors were still in good condition in 1988, and a screened porch at the rear looks down over a deep, shaded back yard in the direction of the Schuylkill River. The exterior walls are stone painted white, masonry being more commonplace than frame in this locality. Inside this comfortable home the musician, his wife, and four children lived for many years.

When Wallace was born on March 2, 1879, his parents and his older sister and brother were still living at 3311 Hamilton Street. Dr. John J. McLeod of 3905 Locust Street was in attendance. Nearly eight weeks later, on April 30, the Gilchrists filed a birth certificate but still had not named the baby.

The earliest surviving photo of Wallace shows him with his sister, Anna. He looks about two or three years old, rather pudgy in the face, his hair very straight down over his forehead and almost covering his ears. In another photo, taken perhaps a year later, both Charles and Anna pose behind Wallace, but he is the only one wearing a hat, a very wide-brimmed affair tilted far back to show the hair covering most of his forehead, and held in place with a string. In both pictures his eyes have a certain dreamy serenity that is never seen in his brother Charles, whose eyes gleam with passionate intensity.

Photographs of the Gilchrist children were carefully posed, the youngsters dressed and groomed for the appointment. In a third picture Wallace again appears a bit dreamy, but also not too pleased with all the dressing up and posing. His older brother, Charles, however, looks rather proud as he holds Teddy and Wallace in the required position. Wallace seems much happier in another picture showing him alone with Teddy, who is still an infant, with both arms around the little boy's middle to hold him upright. In a fourth picture, taken five or six years later, Wallace and Teddy stand outdoors near the top of a flight of steps with a decorative wrought-iron railing. They wear boots laced well above their ankles, and while Teddy is dressed like a sailor, Wallace looks as if he is about to leave for church or dancing class with his neat jacket and trousers, a tie, and a hat sitting at a perfect angle.

Both boys look more than a little impatient to get on to something more exciting. The Gilchrist children were all intelligent, attractive, and very gifted. The three boys were very athletic and highly competitive. Wallace could swim, sail, play tennis—he came within one point of winning a tournament at Prout's Neck—figure-skate, and even do the so-called "giant swing" on the trapeze. He could also climb a telephone pole, as shown by an old snapshot showing him sitting on top of one dressed in jacket and tie, legs and arms arranged in perfect symmetry. In those days, well over a century ago, wearing a jacket and tie meant nothing special. Boys and men did even the sweatiest things dressed formally and would have been flabbergasted by today's mode of dress.

Wallace strove mightily to keep up with his two brothers, especially Charlie, who was six years older and a born athlete. In so doing he made the unhappy discovery that his heart could not always deliver the power he needed to compete. Bill reported that his father's heart developed a leaky valve and a murmur and became enlarged. The timing of this and its cause, whether congenital or caused by a childhood disease, are unknown. Certainly both of his parents lived long lives, his father's stretching over seventy years, his mother's eighty-two years. Not heart disease but severe depression led to his father's death, shortly before Christmas in 1916, and also killed Teddy. Wallace was spared the manic-depressive sufferings of his father and brother and somehow coped with his heart disease well enough to lead a fairly normal life.

Both he and his daughter Peggy, my mother, who also suffered from heart disease, developed a serene outlook on life, in part because of their personalities, but also because serenity prevents heart attacks, and many years spent with a weak heart builds a sharp awareness of how fragile life can be.

Exactly when Wallace began painting is unknown, but in using his family, especially his father, as subjects he soon demonstrated a formidable talent. He had the immense good fortune to have been raised in a family that respected and excelled in the arts, and he lived in a city blessed with the old and venerable Pennsylvania Academy of the Fine Arts, founded in 1806.

In October of 1896, after the worst of Philadelphia's summer heat, Wallace began his studies at the Academy. He was only seventeen years old but had already received instruction and encouragement from Winslow Homer while on summer vacation near Prout's Neck, in Scarborough, Maine. It was now time to begin the long and arduous formal training.

His family had lived at the Wayne Avenue address since he was about seven, so he was undoubtedly familiar with the trolley or train ride to downtown Philadelphia. By today's standards it is only a short commute to the city from Mt. Airy, but in 1896 it required a ride of several miles. By that year the Academy had progressed a long way from its founding, when two-thirds of its shareholders were lawyers and businessmen more intent upon collecting for their museum than on developing a genuine school for artists. For many years, in fact, there existed a strong feeling of hostility and tension between the artists, who did the real work, and the managers and shareholders of the Academy, who made the decisions.

However, as the years passed, the artists began slowly to gain the control they needed. Out of the vast diversity of the American nation came those with the drive, the talent, and the passion to become artists. They were all drawn to this singularly beautiful edifice on Broad Street in Philadelphia. There they settled in for the basic training the school provided. It was in this setting that Wallace began his studies, working under the guidance of some of the great artists of his day, among them Cecilia Beaux, Thomas Anshutz, and William Merritt Chase.

Thomas Eakins, the moving force on the Academy's faculty until 1886, though no longer physically present, had left an enduring legacy. One of the greatest of American painters, Eakins served as a teacher at the Academy and from the beginning fought against the stuffy attitudes of the governing board. By the time he resigned in 1886, supposedly because he insisted that female students be allowed to paint from nude male models, he had ruffled not a few fine feathers. If he was too radical for the administration, a man ahead of his time, he was unquestionably a hero and a powerful stimulus to his pupils.

The school where he taught is situated on Broad Street just a few blocks north of City Hall, where the statue of William Penn perches to watch benignly over the sprawl of modern Philadelphia. In 1898 a circular put out by the Committee on Instruction shows that the Academy wisely arranged for the two seventeen-week terms to run from early October to the end of May, thereby avoiding the worst of the city's sultry summer heat. Classes were held six days a week from 9 A.M. until 10 P.M., and although a student could not take every course offered, it was a heavy work load that Gilchrist undertook.

Before he matriculated at this famous old school, Gilchrist was influenced primarily by the geography, the climate, and the social and cultural life of Philadelphia. For seventeen years he lived in the environs of Philadelphia, making occasional trips with his family to Maine and other vacation spots but returning always to his home base.

Like most great cities, Philadelphia was built on a river, but unlike some of the smaller inland cities and towns, it flourished so well that it spread westward for about two miles until it bumped into another river. Between the Delaware River on the east, which flows between Pennsylvania and New Jersey at that point, and the Schuylkill River on the west lies all of downtown Philadelphia. When the city's westward expansion was stymied by another river, Philadelphia first took the easier course of moving northward, between the two rivers, and southward seven miles to the point where the rivers merge and continue flowing toward Chesapeake Bay and the Atlantic.

The reader who has neither visited the city nor delved into its history may not realize to what extent it dominated the world of pre-Revolutionary America. In a land settled by thousands of adventurers, criminals, explorers, and refugees from the ancient regimes and deeply imbedded intolerances of Europe, Philadelphia was preeminent as the city of tolerance, prosperity, and the pursuit of a better life. In 1682 William Penn, the city's Quaker founder, employed a city planner to lay out the town in a gridiron

*Uncle John*

pattern with City Hall in the geometrical center and with four spacious and shaded squares in each quadrant: Rittenhouse and Logan on the west, and Washington and Franklin on the east, close to the Delaware River. So well conceived was this arrangement, and so successfully did the city attract men and women of intellect, talent, and ambition, that in 1765 a Scottish nobleman visiting the city was moved to call it "perhaps one of the wonders of the world."

In support of this extravagant claim, the Scotsman wrote that considering the "magnificence and diversity of the places of worship, the plenty of provisions brought to market, and the industry of all of its inhabitants, one will not hesitate to call it the first town in America."

If the United States today is a pluralistic society, Philadelphia at the time of the Revolution lay at the very source and foundation of this pluralism. By 1806, when the Pennsylvania Academy was founded, the city already had a proud history of political stability and power, having been the first capital of the new American nation from 1790 to 1800. It was a refuge for the persecuted from all of the faraway lands of the world and from several of the American colonies as well. Its nurture of cultural growth side by side with commercial prosperity, together with its location halfway between New England and the South, made Philadelphia the perfect place for both the junior and senior Gilchrists to build careers in the arts.

On Monday, October 3, 1898, Gilchrist began his third year at the Academy and started the first of two seventeen-week terms that would end on Saturday, May 27, 1899, in time to enjoy Memorial Day. Between the two terms the school allowed no break except the usual Sunday off. A century ago the majority of Americans, artists included, worked a six-day week and rested on the Sabbath. Generous Christmas, mid-winter, or spring vacations were unknown in a world that toiled in bondage to the so-called Protestant work ethic.*

What made it all bearable to Wallace as he worked steadily away to master the techniques of painting was his acquaintance with a woman in Bethlehem, Pennsylvania, a woman who was to enrich his life every bit as much as his work. Her name was Lucretia, and not long after they met he decided he wanted very much to marry her.

*The "Circular of Committee on Instruction" for that academic year lists the following instructors: Thomas P. Anshutz, Cecilia Beaux, Hugh H. Breckenridge, William M. Chase, Charles Grafly, George McClellan, M.D., Will S. Robinson, Henry J. Thouron.

# LUCRETIA

Lucretia Gilchrist was born on January 1, 1880, in Newark, New Jersey, the first child of Bernard deSchweinitz and Ellen Lord, and she passed away eighty-eight years later at her beloved Roadside in East Harpswell, Maine. Her ancestry in the United States is longer and more complex than her husband's. The deSchweinitz family traces back to the founding of the Moravian Church in 1457 by the followers of the martyred John Hus. The von Schweinitz name was carried to North America when Hans Christian Alexander von Schweinitz arrived in Bethlehem, Pennsylvania, on November 16, 1770. On her mother's side, Lucretia was a direct descendant of, and in fact was named for, Lucretia Mott, the famous Quaker feminist and abolitionist, who descended from the Coffins and Folgers who settled Nantucket Island, Massachusetts.

To me, she was simply Grandma, and the very soul of modesty and kindness. Although she lived as a widow for almost forty-two years and suffered from a bad heart in her old age, her youthfulness and will to live were indomitable. A rather small, quiet-spoken lady, she seemed to personify all that was grandmotherly, optimistic, and loving. Yet when the chips were down, as they often were in her long and fascinating life, she became a woman of amazing toughness and grit. As her daughter Peggy, my mother, once put it, "Your grandmother is an amazing woman, Robert. She lives on pills and sheer will power."

Her husband was taken from her by heart disease on November 4, 1926, just two months before she turned forty-seven. At this tragic moment, she had already survived more than her share of trial and tribulation, beginning with her own girlhood. When she was only sixteen, Lucretia's own mother, Ellen Lord deSchweinitz, passed away and left a husband and five young children. Lucretia was suddenly thrust into the role of mother, housekeeper, and companion to her bereaved father, Bernard deSchweinitz, who owned a dairy business in Montrose, Pennsylvania, and whose own mother had traumatized him by dying when he was only eleven. Onto the young and tender shoulders of Lucretia, therefore, fell a heavy burden, for not only did her father lean upon her, but four younger children ranging in age from five to fifteen looked to their older sister to help fill the void. Examining a photo taken of her during this critical period, one sees the sober, unsmiling face of a girl who must now quickly shed the carefree ways of girlhood and make a quantum leap into adulthood.

Kneeling next to her to hold a little dog is Lucretia's only sister, Margaret, then a child of five but later to become a professor of French at Vassar. Margaret may have lost her mother, but she can still crack a smile because she still has a big sister, three older brothers, and a dog. It is no wonder that people admired and loved Lucretia. Her capacity to weather the storm of her mother's death was, unbeknownst to her then, a baptism by fire for the far greater storm that lay thirty years into the future.

Lucretia met Wallace in Maine during the summer, not long after he had met and fallen under the spell of Winslow Homer at Prout's Neck. Next to his own parents, there was probably no other pair of people in Wallace's short life span who so profoundly affected and influenced him as Lucretia deSchweinitz and Winslow Homer. Perhaps it was these two encounters that inspired in him such a feeling for Maine and that gave the impetus for the family's move to East Harpswell in 1915. In any case he and Lucretia wasted no time falling in love, and by the time Wallace set sail for Europe in September 1900, they were engaged.

The story of Wallace's proposal to Lucretia is the only truly personal story she ever confided to me. Lucretia must have known instinctively that she could impart this confidence to me without losing her natural dignity or my respect. In any case, when she took me aside she sounded almost like a giddy school girl sharing a secret, and I am sure I was too astonished by her revelation to do much more than smile and store it away in my memory.

She began by telling me how deeply in love she was with Wallace and he with her, yet she wanted to be sure before she gave her consent. She was coy and wily enough not to make herself too easy a conquest, though in truth her heart had melted for him long before that moment. When she told him she needed time to think it over, she almost pitied him for the forlorn look that crossed his face. He must have felt the agony of anxiety that seizes a man at such a moment, unable to realize that Lucretia had no intention of refusing him. She was already his, and the only thing that excused her little ploy was the joy she gave him when she accepted.

I will never know whether she told me this story because she felt like sharing or because she thought to teach me a little of the ways of women. Many years passed before I realized that she could fool anyone into thinking she was just another sweet old lady with no ulterior motive for anything she said or did. Most people, myself foremost among them, fell under her spell and went away happy.

*Portrait of Lucretia*

www.meyersphoto.com

Lucretia's life as an artist's wife was never smooth or easy, never truly secure, but when Wallace died the road ahead must have looked perilous indeed. He left no money to speak of, being inclined to enjoy it when he had it, no life insurance, and probably a handful of unpaid bills. Social Security was not there as a safety net, for it took a national catastrophe in the Great Depression to give rise to this rather revolutionary idea. All she had, therefore, were family, friends, and her own inner resources. As it turned out, she survived and was able to see beyond the immediate crisis and to take hope from the generosity of a devoted member of her own family.

It was Lucretia's own aunt who came to the rescue. Aunt Lucretia, sister of the mother who had died in 1896, had married a wealthy New York retailer, and she must have persuaded her husband, Albert Strauss, to set aside some of his holdings in a trust fund sufficient to provide the artist's family with some solid and reliable income. When the news of this generosity reached the newly widowed Lucretia Gilchrist, she probably wept with relief. She and her children were suddenly given new hope by an act of compassion and love.

Lucretia, being an optimistic child of the nineteenth century, was always one to adapt to changing circumstances and glean enjoyment from her every life experience.

Raised during the Gay Nineties and married during the euphoria of America's so-called Coming of Age, she lived in a time of great hope in the long struggle for mankind's progress, for freedom from the awful scourges of famine, pestilence, disease, and war. Science at that time was perceived as an ever growing army advancing invincibly to defeat these scourges, especially in the field of medicine, where unfortunately the so-called miracle drugs arrived too late to save Wallace. On the other hand, were it not for the skillful ministrations of one of the better known cardiologists in Philadelphia, Dr. Joseph Vanderveer, neither Peggy nor Lucretia would have lived as long as they did.

Wallace lived just one generation too early to benefit from the new miracle drugs introduced just prior to World War II. Because of his untimely death he lacked sufficient time to complete his tasks, one of which was to provide security for his family and the other to assimilate the vast, chaotic revolution churning through the conventions of the art world. A lifetime of forty-seven years was not long enough for him to produce enough work to constitute a "normal" career. By contrast, most of his contemporaries lived at least twenty years longer.

Unlike his friend and mentor Winslow Homer, who was senior to him by some forty-three years, Wallace never made the total and exclusive commitment to painting that would have cost him the joys and distractions of a wife and children. By contrast, Homer decided after an early and unsatisfactory love affair that if a woman could not adapt herself to his work and the demands it placed on him, there would simply be no married life for him. His young friend Wallace, however, fell deeply in love with a very special woman and never regretted marrying her. In fact, it could be justifiably argued that meeting Lucretia made Wallace what he was, and that without her he never could have achieved what he did. Because these two artists, one old enough to be a grandfather to the other, had such different temperaments, the paths they took and the reputations they earned stand in stark contrast.

In 1926 Wallace's only son and namesake turned sixteen just two months before his father's death. He was a tall, husky son of Maine born on Cliff Island, just east of Portland in Casco Bay. The family called him Bill, and he soon became the cause of great concern to his mother. One of the schools he attended after his father died was the Nazareth Military Academy in Nazareth, Pennsylvania. This school was a most unpleasant situation for a lad accustomed to life near the seacoast with friends he had known for many years. (Bill was not quite five when the family moved to Maine from Philadelphia.) Before many months had passed, Bill let his family know just how strongly he objected to his new circumstances. In January of 1927 he took a brief, highly unauthorized leave from the regimen of the military school by hitchhiking back up to Maine.

Meanwhile, his mother was living in Philadelphia, secure in the belief that each of her three children was in a particular place doing a particular thing. Her security dissolved when a newspaper printed a brief item announcing that the son of the late W. W. Gilchrist had landed safely on the mainland after having been marooned for three days on Ragged Island in the middle of a January blizzard!

As Bill told the story, however, it sounded more like a marvelous adventure than a serious breach of discipline. He and a school chum from Brunswick simply rowed the six or so miles out to Ragged, home at one time of poet Edna St. Vincent Millay, fully expecting to return home the same day. With them they took a shotgun, some raisins, matches, a small ax, and not much else. Ragged was the same island to which Bill had rowed alone, before breakfast, against family rules, when he was a twelve-year-old. Something about the island roused and challenged him, luring him to row across the freezing winter sea to a place he knew well. It all seemed harmless enough and exhilarating until the boys, having dragged their twelve-foot skiff across a mile of ice and rowed the rest of the way, arrived at Ragged as a storm was brewing. Even worse, the storm showed signs of being a three-day nor'easter.

The cellar of an old house provided shelter, and the boys set about cutting a hole in the ceiling to let out the smoke of the fire they started. They split up some doors to provide firewood, they melted ice for drinking water, and when the raisins were eaten they found some frozen cranberries. The storm was throwing a spectacular surf across the entire tip of the island, but by the third day, with the boys famished for food, the wind abated enough for Bill to try getting through the surf in their skiff to a nearby lobster trap. His friend thought Bill would drown for sure, but somehow he got back to shore with two lobsters. On the fourth day the wind shifted around to the west and the boys were able to row to the nearest land some three miles away.

*Lucretia as a young girl*

Many years later Lucretia still worried about her son, and for good reason. By 1964 he had been married three times and fathered five children, two of them by his third wife, who committed suicide that year. Soon thereafter Bill experienced what may have been the single luckiest encounter of his life when he met Bette Butterworth. They were married on April 27, 1965, and Bill's two little sons were given a new mother, who did a superlative job of raising them. Immediately after their marriage, however, Lucretia realized what a formidable task Bette had undertaken, for Bill came to this marriage with a full blown manic-depressive condition that would take all of Bette's considerable tact and energy to handle.

On a visit to Gladwyne, Pennsylvania, to see his sister Peggy, Bill and his new bride spent a few hours with Lucretia, who lived in Germantown in Priestly House, a Unitarian home for the aged. The scene as they finally prepared to leave for home in White Plains, New York, is one Bette remembered well. Bill had gone out to load the car and Peggy was walking her guests out through the kitchen to the back door. Lucretia walked up to the back door, and just when Bette expected her to begin the always protracted ritual of saying good-bye, she suddenly turned around and looked rather soulfully at her fourth daughter-in-law. With both hands she reached out and held tightly onto Bette's. "Take care of my boy," she said.

Fortunately for Lucretia, her daughters were not as much of a problem, being both older and more self-sufficient. However, for a while Lucretia wasn't sure she could afford to keep the farmhouse in Harpswell. At one point she even put it on the market, and the story is told that a woman interested in buying property in the area appeared one day when Lucretia was out of town and asked a neighbor, Mrs. Leeman, if she could borrow the key to see the house.

"Absolutely not," replied Mrs. Leeman.

"And why not, may I ask? All I want to do is take a quick look around."

"Not while I have the key you won't. That place ain't for sale. Don't you know who lives there?"

"Of course I know. The Gilchrists."

"Well, now, don't you realize the Gilchrist family is an institution here in East Harpswell? You can't just go buyin' up a place like that!"

"Well, I never!" said the woman and drove away much offended. The Gilchrists came that close to selling Roadside.

Although Lucretia continued to face the difficult task of raising a fatherless teenage son, she was not the stern and struggling widow who never took any respite from her daily round of chores. She was able to extract from every day and place and experience a kind of spiritual sustenance that kept her heart pumping and her hopes high. When she was first widowed she had to maintain Roadside, which fortunately she owned outright, and to see to her children's futures, but the question that must have concerned her most was where, with whom, and at what cost she could spend the long winter months when Roadside was empty. In winter the old farmhouse, even with the furnace Wallace himself had installed, was virtually uninhabitable without a strong man to do the lifting, hauling, and shoveling.

During the year after Wallace died she was first taken in by one of the McKeen sisters, a member of one of the oldest Brunswick families, in whose house at the corner of Maine and McKeen the Gilchrists had spent their first winter in Maine in 1915-1916. It was the dining room of this old house that the artist had captured so beautifully in a piece he called *The Gilchrist Family at Breakfast* (not to be confused with *After Breakfast*, painted in 1925 at Roadside).

Lucretia stayed a short while in the McKeen house but moved down to the city of Bethlehem, north of Philadelphia, later that winter to act as a companion to an elderly woman. She would have felt right at home there, where she had lived as a girl, after her father sold his dairy business in Montrose and went to work for Bethlehem Steel. The woman died within the year, however, and Lucretia then found she could move down to Philadelphia and live with her own mother-in-law, Susan Beaman Gilchrist. Wallace's mother, widowed since 1916, lived in a tiny apartment on the second floor of one of those charming little brick houses that still survive, somehow, under the shadows of the giant new towers that fill the sky just a few blocks north.

For Lucretia it was a cozy arrangement because on the ground floor were the offices of her brother-in-law, the prominent architect Edmund Beaman Gilchrist, Wallace's younger brother. It was perfectly natural for Susan to invite her daughter-in-law to share her quarters. The senior Mrs. Gilchrist had by then been a widow for ten years and would have warmly welcomed Lucretia's company. During those heady years between 1926 and 1931, while the nation careened toward the Crash and the ensuing catastrophe of the Great Depression, Lucretia and her mother-in-law were in residence in the little house on Latimer Street, and one can imagine a rather busy life for the two of them.

Though separated by some thirty-three years, they had much in common. If Lucretia could tell stories about her childhood, for in those days people were entertained more by each other than by the media, certainly Susan Beaman Gilchrist, having been one of seventeen children, would have had some fairly good stories of her own to tell. Her father had been a minister of the Swedenborgian Church and supposedly remarked that having so many children was like "making angels for Heaven." The cause of death of the first is unknown, but the bearing and raising of nine children may have contributed. His second wife bore him five boys and three girls.

On July 17, 1931, Susan Beaman Gilchrist passed away in the middle of her eighty-third year. Again Lucretia was forced to readjust her living arrangements, but not for long. Wallace's only sister, Anna Redelia Gilchrist, who had never found the man of her dreams, or perhaps after a time had stopped searching, was in that year sixty years old while Lucretia was fifty-one. Both women felt a deep love and concern for the family. Both had loved Wallace and still loved his memory. The children were now twenty-one (Bill), twenty-five (Nelly), and twenty-seven (Peggy). Nelly had decided to begin a career in sculpture while Peggy had graduated from Russell Sage College and was working as a dietitian at Whitman's Cafeteria in downtown Philadelphia. Bill was a carpenter working on the houses his Uncle Teddy was designing for the real estate tycoon George Woodward in the fashionable suburbs just north of the city. With all the family living in the area, then, it was natural for Lucretia and Anna (known as Aunt Nancy) to pool their resources and live together. The apartment they found was at 1906 Sansom Street, just a few blocks north and west of the little house on Latimer Street and a short walk from Rittenhouse Square.

Philadelphia in 1931 was of course not the same as Philadelphia in 1927. The four intervening years had been unnerving for almost all Americans, and even the most casual students of American history will remember that the United States was paralyzed by the fear and suffering that Franklin Roosevelt referred to in his first inaugural address when he said, "The only thing we have to fear is fear itself. . . ." However, owing to the generosity of Lucretia and Albert Strauss, it is doubtful that the two Gilchrist ladies, Anna and Lucretia, lived in fear of poverty. What must have worried them, after family concerns, was the need to put some distance between their new residence on Sansom Street and the decay enveloping the city as the flight to the suburbs slowly but surely emptied Philadelphia of its middle and upper class residents.

*Lucretia as a young woman*

No records were kept by the family of the costs of living in those days, although Lucretia did keep a very abbreviated listing of her expenses and some shorthand notations of her social activities in four compact little books entitled "The Universal Household Expense Book." However, with the knowledge we now have of the economic history of these years, we can easily deduce that with so many businesses failing, banks closing, and the consequent rise in unemployment to approximately 25% of the work force, the prices that had been driven up in the Roaring Twenties by a freely expanding money supply and the speculative frenzy of Wall Street would have collapsed in many sectors of Philadelphia's economy. Perhaps rentals had also fallen, so that if Lucretia's trust fund had been wisely invested, she might even have been able to save a little.

In any case, the influx of poor Blacks from the South, the nationwide migration from farm to city begun after the Civil War, and the colossal movement to America during those seventy odd years of the dispossessed of Europe and Asia—all of these vast, churning upheavals had begun finally to affect the quaint little streets of Philadelphia. Yet nearly seventy years after Lucretia and Anna first moved to 1906 Sansom Street, the brick apartment building is still standing. Lucretia lived there from 1931 until the early sixties, spending her summers at Roadside, where she renewed herself with visits from children, grandchildren, great-grandchildren, and friends.

She had ten grandchildren, all of whom would visit her at Roadside during their summer vacations, some with parents, some without. She was a woman in her sixties then and with more than her share of infirmities, including serious heart problems, so she had to keep her wits about her when two or more of her six grandsons arrived simultaneously for a visit. On one memorable occasion she returned to the farmhouse from a shopping trip in her green 1941 Ford sedan (in which she was said to terrorize half the Harpswells with her cavalier disregard for speed limits and right of way), only to find two small grandsons struggling on the kitchen floor in what appeared to be mortal combat. Not the least bit daunted, she placed her parcels on the kitchen counter, walked over to the two grunting, writhing little savages, reached down until she had each of her hands firmly entwined in a grandson's hair and applied a steady upward pressure. After they stopped yelping and begged her for mercy, she stood them against the kitchen wall and quietly explained that any more fighting would mean no more fish chowder for the rest of their vacation. Such was the reputation of Grandma's fish chowder that there was instant compliance, and two of the sweetest little dears a grandmother could wish for began to put away the food.

She lived very much in the present and took a girlish delight in keeping up with the world, especially the world of crossword puzzles and professional baseball. Crossword puzzles were a private pleasure for her, but baseball was public and encompassed the radio and the attention of whoever was visiting, especially as the pennant race tightened after Labor Day. One granddaughter recalls vividly how excited this otherwise sedate and dignified woman became during a ball game heard on her little Philco radio set perched on the table in the dining room. When the Red Sox, or perhaps the Phillies or Connie Mack's Athletics, scored a home run, Grandma would scream and shout like a teenager, and if her team won she would dance around the house with her granddaughter until the spell wore off.

Those long, wonderful summer days spent in the place she and Wallace had loved so much would have brought back memories stretching all the way back to 1915. Such was the magnetic pull of that little farmhouse on the seacoast that none of her maladies could ever keep her away from Roadside in the summer. When she was too frail to take the long journey north by train, there was always a friend or relative to drive her.

So it was that in June of 1968 this grandson drove from Connecticut down to Philadelphia, to Priestly House, the Unitarian home for the aged in Germantown, where Lucretia had moved from Sansom Street to spend her last years. She was eighty-eight years old and beaming with pleasure and anticipation when I packed her things into the car and drove her north. After spending the night in Greenwich, where she briefly renewed acquaintance with two very small great-granddaughters, she was installed in the car of her son-in-law from Stamford, who drove her on the last leg of her trip to Maine. When we kissed her good-bye that sunny June morning, we promised we'd see her in August at Roadside, for we all adored the little farmhouse by the sea, and we all adored Grandma. Everyone did.

When the news came ten days later that Grandma, having safely reached Roadside, had suddenly taken ill and died, her two newest great-granddaughters took the news with barely a moistened eye. For all the rest of us, though, those who had felt the quiet strength, the boundless optimism, and the tender love of this dear lady, the loss was like the sudden wilting of flowers after a May snowstorm. To have known this sweet woman, if only now and then, was to understand how perfectly she had been able to give her husband the love and devotion he needed to carry through his life's work.

*Three generations of W. W. Gilchrists: The musician, the grandson, and the artist.*

## LIKE FATHER, LIKE SON?

**W**allace's father was possessed of great energy, creative power, and intellect, and in his sheer determination to bring classical music to Philadelphia in a big and lasting way, his accomplishments were formidable. As a musician and composer, one of the founders of the Philadelphia Orchestra and a prominent church choir conductor, he was a major cultural figure in Philadelphia.

As a human being, he was far from the stereotype of the awesome and dictatorial Victorian father. By all accounts, he was a gentle and loving spirit who wanted the best for his children and worked terribly hard to help pave the way for their successes. He was in the tradition of many Americans, especially those newly arrived on these shores, who hunger for the reality of the American dream of wealth, security, and fame, and who feel that if a family is to progress from one generation to the next, sacrifices may be called for and should gladly be made.

The senior W. W. Gilchrist was the ideal father for a boy like Wallace, willing to give much of himself to his family when he was often bedeviled by a lack of time to do what he wanted most, compose great music. Although he was revered for his enormous contributions to the music world, according to his own lights he never fulfilled his deepest yearning for creative greatness. Without ever having met anyone who knew him, one may be certain that in his prime he was a magnificent man. Yet he was at times inwardly tortured by his failure to achieve the impossible, but simultaneously too kindly to subject people to his melancholy.

That such a load of repressed discouragement did not hamper him more than it did was probably due to his strength of character, but there was a woman in his life who

www.meyersphoto.com

*Deer in Winter Woods*

loved him and indulged and understood him as no one else did. She was his wife, Susan Beaman Gilchrist, whom he called Maudie. She must have had her hands full with this complex and driven man, but she stood with him, raised their children, and was always there when he needed her. It was always the wife and mother who quietly held the Gilchrists together, and this devotion was repeated in the marriage of Wallace and Lucretia.

The senior Gilchrist was a full thirty-three years older than the infant to whom he and Maudie finally decided to give his own name, and there was something magically prophetic in this decision, almost as if, in gazing into the face of his third child, the father saw a reflection of himself and his own spirit. Unless new letters are miraculously unearthed by a distant family connection, Wallace's first years in the big house at 5914 Wayne Avenue in Germantown are fated to be a blank spot in this chronicle.

On March 2, 1879, Wallace was ushered into the Gilchrist family, and into what seemed for a while to be anonymity. When the family finally filed a birth certificate for their brand new son, on April 30, eight weeks after his birth, his first name was conspicuously absent from the document. Any number of reasons might account for this omission. Was he not expected to live? Was there a family quarrel over the choice of a name? Or were the Gilchrists simply so busy they hadn't thought of a name and wanted to wait and see what people might suggest? Perhaps the musician and his wife wanted to be very sure before they placed the name of the original W. W. Gilchrist on yet another generation, knowing it could become as much of a burden as an impetus to the child.

As the years went by, the anonymous infant was first called Waddie, then Wally, and on formal occasions Wallace. Such was this little lad's nature, and such was his eminent and bearded father, that the name W. W. Gilchrist became more of a destiny than a name, and Wallace became less an ordinary lad born to a genteel family in late nineteenth-century Philadelphia than a little spirit on whom the Bestower of talents had laid a fabulous gift, and whose destiny was to unfold accordingly.

Late in May of 1886, W. W. Gilchrist, Sr., set sail with a group of friends for a two-month tour of Europe, beginning with the British Isles. It was the musician's first trip to the Old World, and he faithfully and rather elegantly recorded his impressions in a long diary and in lengthy letters to his wife and children.

He was himself the grandson of the first W. W. Gilchrist to migrate from Scotland to North America, and though he was much captivated by the English and their unfailing kindness and courtesy, he must have felt an especially strong affinity for the Scots.

His wife stayed behind in Philadelphia to manage a large household with four children: Anna was fifteen, Charlie thirteen, Wally seven, and little Teddy just a year old. In 1886 a woman's place was still very much in the home. Who's to say, in any case, that Maudie wasn't secretly delighted to spend some time alone with her children and friends while her famous husband went off for the Grand Tour and a richly deserved vacation.

The trip was exciting and memorable as well as far more exhausting than he had anticipated, but the traveling musician, who was now a man of forty, still managed after long days of travel by stagecoach, on horseback, on the train, and on foot to find the energy to keep a diary and write long letters home, one of which he composed for his seven-year-old son Waddie. This is the only existing letter of a personal and revealing nature written from Senior to Junior. Aside from the picture it gives of a man speaking over a wide gap of years to a bright little boy who happens to be his son, and who may well be in his heart of hearts his pride and joy, the letter also adds two illuminating clues to Wallace's talent.

First, and almost parenthetically, when discussing a new picture book of locomotives, he interrupts himself to say, "You must not draw too much though—I think you ought to be running out now—not drawing—keep the locomotive book for next winter." A bit farther on, as he talks about the churches destroyed by the English, as well as the existing abbeys and cathedrals where choir boys perform two services a day, he says the buildings "are magnificent and I am getting photographs of them, so that you can copy some perhaps."

It is perfectly clear that Wallace at age seven was already flexing his fingers and honing his skills as a draughtsman, and such was his enthusiasm that he would often rather draw than go "running out" into the sultry June air to play.* After all, here was the tantalizing complexity of a new locomotive just begging to be rendered on paper, and when Pops got back from his trip he would have some wonderful photos of the cathedrals. How they ever made all that ponderous stone stand so tall and soar so high was a wonder, and the way to understand it was to pursue with your pencil and pen every line and space until it became clear. Then it was something to show the family, something even Charlie would admire. Anna was always sweet with him anyway, and of course the baby only wanted to touch and tear at it, but Charlie was the one who would smile or frown.

How fascinating it would have been to use a modern camcorder to film the scene where Maudie sits with Waddie and reads him Pops's letter. In any case, whether Waddie stayed inside to draw locomotives and cathedrals or went out to play, the musician's concern for the boy's physical and social development tells us as much about the father as it does about his  son. Wally, in the eyes of his father, was more than simply a rapidly developing artistic genius. He was therefore to be cautioned against staying indoors too much. There was a whole world of outdoor fun and games, woods and animals, sports and competitions and skills to be learned. There were friends to be made and things to try and dare. It was summer in Germantown and time for all little boys to be "running out."

In the rough and tumble of a boyhood sandwiched between a brilliant and gallant older brother and a little brother who would one day become a hugely successful architect, Wally followed his own star and found the material pickings a whole lot leaner than he had hoped for. If his distinguished father, soaking up the ancient atmosphere among all the ghosts of the carefully preserved abbeys and cathedrals which he so loved to contemplate, understood and was fully aware of Wally's talent, there is no mention of it anywhere in his letters.

However, one passage from the letter does throw more light on the growth of the artistic spirit in Wallace's childhood. This passage is especially revealing both as to the father's conception of beauty, and as an indication, ever so slight and parenthetical, that there really wasn't such a large gap between father and son after all, especially in matters of the aesthetic. Having recently visited some old abbeys, the father writes that their ruins are overgrown with ivy, broken and worn by storm and age and altogether very beautiful on one clear, moonlit night. At this point he says to his son, "I think even a little fellow like you would have said it was beautiful."

The senior Gilchrist was acutely aware of his own lack of great material success. He therefore fervently wished for his sons to obtain what he felt he lacked. In this hope he was partially satisfied, for at least one son, Teddy, did very well financially. More important from posterity's viewpoint is the record of achievement of the three brothers, each in a field directly or indirectly related to art. Teddy was known as the most artistic architect on the East Coast, while Charlie for eight years was partner in a small civil engineering firm in Philadelphia before leaving to venture as an engineer in the Philippines and as a pioneer in motion pictures on the West Coast, not to mention his brilliant exploits as an intrepid mountaineer.

*Pencil Sketch*, 3 x 5"

Wally's achievements were never measured in dollars while he was alive. Afflicted as he was with chronic and worsening heart disease throughout most of his adulthood, what is amazing about him is the magnitude and beauty of the work he created. Only a tiny handful of his contemporaries in the field of painting lived shorter lives. A quick survey of the life spans of ninety prominent European and American artists (all but two born in the nineteenth century) reveals that seventy-two of them lived beyond age sixty. Even more amazing is that despite the primitive state of medicine then, fourteen of these seventy-two survived into their eighties, five into their nineties, and one (Turner) made it to one hundred. Gilchrist is one of only nine who did not make it to fifty. Evidently artists were a healthy lot.

The senior Gilchrist was never until the very last months of his life so preoccupied with himself that he overlooked or neglected his three sons and their older sister. They were not the sort of children that one could easily overlook, either as a parent or as a friend of the family. The three brothers, cheered on by their parents and their older sister Anna, were always striving to fulfill their separate destinies as sons of a great Philadelphian, and as American men trying to deal with the great dream of success.

All of them did very well, and certainly no one could have been prouder than their dad to hear, year after year, of their struggles and accomplishments. Yet this wonderful father became so disappointed in his own apparently barren production of music in the latter part of his life that nothing could help it. All the applause, all the testimonial dinners and concerts of his work, the beautifully written mementos presented to him, even the delights of being a grandfather and babysitting little Nelly and her older sister Peggy on Cliff Island, Maine, could not dispel the cloud that closed over him as he neared his seventieth birthday. He enjoyed some wonderfully triumphant moments, but as he came to accept that he was not destined for the greatness of a

Mozart or a Beethoven, he slowly lost his hold on the dream and promise that had taken him so far. The fire died out, and life was suddenly very empty. He lapsed into a long and tragic melancholy that persisted until his death of heart failure just nineteen days before his seventy-first birthday. It was not quite a slow suicide, yet it seems inexplicable that such a wonderfully accomplished and beloved man could have ended this way.

Both Gilchrist and his father were deeply serious men. They were neither jaded cynics nor easygoing comics. Life was not an absurd, tragic, or futile experience. Rather it was a gift from God. It was an opportunity that came just once for the joy of fulfillment in this world. They lived in a land still bursting with raw energy, unfinished tasks, and endless possibilities. In all the arts America knew it had far to go before realizing its full potential, even as it was fast eclipsing the Old World as a fabulous new center of wealth and power.

*Pencil Sketch,* 5 x 7"

Both men knew only too well that for the arts to flourish, people with money, power, and influence had to be educated and excited about their own native artists. Europe and the Orient still had far too much sway over the American art world. In both men, the patriotic strand was woven into their self-images as artists, which explains the frustration and disgust with which Wallace greeted the arrival of the new abstract paintings from Europe, especially France. Not only was this work ugly and unworthy in his eyes, but it also did not express an American sensibility.

The painter also had some strong feelings about other artists and their work, most of which are known only through the letters he wrote his father during his first trip abroad in 1900–1901. As with most first reactions to any new trend in painting, they were a bit hasty and unfair. In 1900 he was a very young man freshly graduated from the Pennsylvania Academy, newly engaged to Lucretia, and wanting nothing so much as to get on with his career and begin his marriage. The last thing he wanted was to explore a whole new mode of painting, especially when he could see in it no real beauty or artistic merit. He and his father had a feeling for beauty that they might have been hard pressed to explain,  but it was a traditional and high-minded view. Innovation for the sake of being different or attracting attention was of no interest to them.

Had Wallace lived another thirty-five years, instead of dying at forty-seven, who knows what direction his work would have taken. Perhaps he would have borrowed some of the techniques invented by the abstractionists, but not unless he could have found some way to enhance the beauty of his work. After all, he had a clientele to please and a family to feed. He did receive gifts from people who admired his work, but never on a regular basis. He never achieved the freedom to explore the frontiers of painting that comes from financial independence.

*The earliest known drawings he did are reproduced here as examples of the talent he showed as a youth. One was penciled on a small card (about 3" x 5") and inserted into the paper pocket of a round cloth-covered frame. On the back side in Wallace's hand in ink are the words "Merry Christmas Aunt Anna From Wallace." Someone has written in pencil the date, 1891, when Wallace was just twelve years old. The second drawing is larger (about 5" x 7") and also sits in a cloth-covered frame. Both drawings may have been copied from books he found at home.

Unlike his father, who was forty when he first toured Europe, Wallace was only twenty-one when he set sail on the S. S. *Statendam* late in September of 1900. Having finished his studies at the Pennsylvania Academy in the spring of that year, he had spent the summer painting and was now intent upon seeing Europe and copying the work of Franz Hals and Diego Velásquez.

The letters he wrote his father on this memorable trip mention three traveling companions, a Dr. Henderson and two fellow painters whose first names were Harry and Joe. Harry was Harry Rittenberg, and of the two painters Harry was the more congenial and spent several months sharing quarters with Wallace in Haarlem while Joe went his separate way, drawn especially to the Exposition in Paris.

Although Wallace wrote many letters to Lucretia, she did not allow personal papers to lie about and probably kept them hidden away. Just a few postcards (stamped with a double "0" to show they were sent while Wallace was in Holland in the fall of 1900) survived the years. The letters and postcards he sent his father, however, are plentiful. He seems to have felt freer to confide in his father than many a son might have, especially in those more formal, Victorian times. It is clear that what Wallace wants from the trip is to get the maximum professional benefit from his time abroad so that he can return to Philadelphia and begin both his married and professional life. He misses Lucretia intensely but realizes that a successful mission in Europe is the best way to be sure that when he sees her again he will be ready to support her and raise a family with her.

While at sea Wallace avoids seasickness and attributes this to "some little laxative pills" that Dr. Henderson brought along, which Wallace takes every night. His ten days on the North Atlantic are spent in conversations with the same people, which he finds tedious after a while, in eating from a table he calls "good but too fancy by far," and in listening to some women "play the piano very well and entertain us every night."

Despite these distractions he finds the ocean a "horribly lonely place—no boats, no anything but water." Much of his time must have been spent musing about the next few months, and at one point he evidently considered staying abroad a year or two. "Perhaps," he says wistfully, "Anna and Lucretia can come over in June and all come home together in August or September. But dear knows, there is no use trying to plan so far ahead. I might stay two years and I might come home in six months."

Wallace writes that if his father wants to know more about the first nine days of the Atlantic crossing, he should ask Lucretia. Wallace had written to her every day since weighing anchor in New York but was too dizzy to write anyone else. In this thought and repeatedly throughout the thirteen letters and two postcards that remain, Wallace makes clear that marrying Lucretia and launching his career are virtually indistinguishable in his mind as his ship plows toward Europe.

There is also just a hint now and then of his nearly lifelong anxiety about his health, but on Monday, October 1, 1900, he reports in a postscript to his letter to the "Folks" in Philadelphia that "we are passing the south of England! It is a grand clear day and all is well. I have never felt in better health in my life, and I have been well the whole way and enjoyed it. It certainly has been a glorious trip. Tomorrow evening we reach Rotterdam."

Distances are short, the terrain flat, and travel easy, so Wallace progresses fairly quickly from Rotterdam, where he and his friends disembark on Tuesday, October 2. They move on to The Hague, where they remain just long enough for Wallace to collect enough impressions to compare it with Amsterdam, their next stop, about thirty miles northeast. "The Hague," he remarks in a postcard to Lucretia, "is more fashionable, very American in dress, and the architecture is more modern."

By that Friday they are enjoying Amsterdam, and Wallace sends a second card to Lucretia showing a beautiful dining room complete with an elaborate chandelier, enormous fernlike plants, and a high arched roof of glass suspended on a delicate tracery of steel. With his exquisite penmanship he squeezes in this message: "This is where we board for 75¢ a night and get a good roast beef dinner for 28¢—beer 6¢ extra. I hate it but drink a little."

*Moonlight at Sea*

On Saturday Wallace travels about ten miles east of Amsterdam to hunt for rooms in the Dutch city of Haarlem, where Franz Hals did so much of his great painting and where entire galleries are filled with his works. Wallace, who has come so far just to see and learn from these masterpieces, and Harry, whom he finds a better companion than Joe, decide to share a place for $20 a month, which includes washing all but their collars. Joe is evidently drawn to Paris, so by Tuesday, October 9, Wallace and Harry are settled in a pension and are looking for a studio, though in a town where little English is spoken they find it difficult to locate any other artists. In fact they find none at all.

Wallace finds the people "slow, heavy, and thick headed," and he reports seeing not one pretty girl or good looking man since he arrived. He goes even further, saying he has yet to see "one person here who even showed signs of having any brains to speak of," although the very poorest seem to live pretty well. His letters overflow with enthusiasm for Franz Hals, however. "If ever there was a painter," he writes on October 7, "it was Franz Hals. He is The man of men. I never knew that such art could exist, it is beyond even what I had imagined—the color is so grand that you can't comprehend till you have visited the paintings several times." He concludes by saying, "His drawing is absolute—and his technique is perfection itself. There is nothing morbid about him—he painted people in a good humor and in brilliant colors. I'm going to settle in Haarlem."

Soon after mailing this letter off to Pops he receives his first letter from home, and this so pleases and excites him that he sits right down to answer it. Although he dates

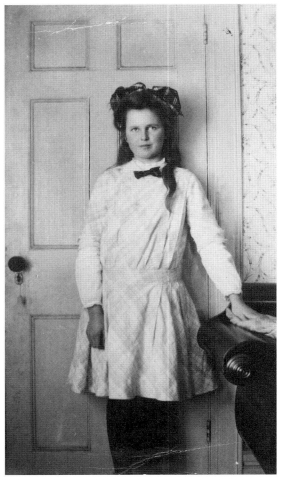

Photographic study for *Girl in White*

it October 9, a Tuesday, he stretches it out for another week before finally completing it on the sixteenth. In this letter, one of his longer ones, he again enthuses about Hals: "Hals is the most encouraging painter—by gum! It is simply tremendous—absolutely the kind of work for me. Rembrandt himself with all his grandeur and light and depth of feeling is a little awkward in handling and clumsy in drawing in comparison to Hals sometimes. I wonder that we don't hear more of Hals. However that has nothing to do with it—Hals is the man to study and I'm going to stay here and do it. Joe says it is no place to stay and has gone to Paris. He says there are no other artists here and that is true, not one. But Hals is here with nine huge canvasses so here I stay and I have got permission to copy. I can't realize that these great things are actually right here and I can see them every day."

Apparently Pops has made Wallace some heartening promises about money, and since the stark limitations of his budget are always just offstage in his mind, he is elated to be able to focus on his goals without the nagging worry of support. We know at this point that he has done at least one portrait rather recently because he proceeds to instruct Pops that if "anyone by some miraculous chance should offer to buy that portrait at a good price, sell it to them of course, but I am not at all pleased with it as a whole—the head and one hand are pretty good but that is all. I think I shall write to Mr. A'Beckett." This statement is typical of Wallace, for he is ever the self-critic, refusing to accept any praise he feels is mere flattery and holding himself to a standard of perfection.

Wallace's remarks about the Dutch reveal a vein of patriotism, or is it homesickness? American girls, he says, have "that taste and grace and refinement and delicacy so characteristic of—well perhaps I am thinking of one girl but no, the Americans are the people" while "even the higher class of women here are frightfully awkward and clumsy in comparison to ours."

He then goes on for a paragraph about the frustration of being in Europe without Lucretia, of wanting sometimes to give up in disgust and "take the next boat home, but—it would do no good—I couldn't have her. The only reason I am here is that I think it will bring us together quicker. Suppose I come home next June or September—

*Girl in White*

www.meyersphoto.com

will people want their portraits painted? And will they come to me? What chance do you think there is of our being married by a year from this winter? It surely couldn't go longer."

By the sixteenth he has begun his copying work and feels better about life. Before signing off on this letter he assures Pops that he indulges in only two extravagances, postage stamps and candy. The rest of that week is presumably spent sitting before the great Hals paintings. On Sunday he and Harry decide to go to Paris to see the great Exposition of 1900.

At the end of a week in the French capital, Wallace has formed some strong opinions about both the exposition and the city. His chief conclusion, after going through the exhibition, is that the American painters are the best, with perhaps Belgium and Holland next in line. The French, he says, have "acres of the darndest trash you ever saw." He is also thoroughly unimpressed by modern Paris but finds ancient Paris fascinating, a theme running through all of his reactions to the great European cities. He feels the chief benefit for him of all the weary hours spent trudging through miles and miles of galleries is the vindication of his belief that "America is ahead and that the painters I have always admired are the painters—Homer, Whistler, Sargent, Chase, etc." He spends a lot of time in the Louvre, and though he admits he has barely begun to see it all, "Giorgione, Titian, Veronese, and Botticelli impressed I think most of all. As for Rubens, I'd rather own that one Giorgione or the one Botticelli than all the Rubens in the world. But they are great no doubt."

Throughout the fall and early winter of 1900 Wallace remains in Haarlem, probably spending most of his time copying in the Hals museum. In his December 17 letter to his father, he says, "Things are the same as ever here. Except that I see more in Hals than I ever did before." In the same letter, a fairly short one for him, he also reveals a certain homesickness for Philadelphia, saying he wrote to Lucretia telling her to make a "great effort to hear . . . all the great music that is going on." Having said this he adds the remark which so perfectly characterizes Lucretia: "She knows how to keep up her spirits, doesn't she!" What he doesn't mention is something he was certainly thinking, that Lucretia also keeps up Wallace's spirits. It is hard to exaggerate the extent to which Wallace has already become emotionally committed to Lucretia, even at the tender age of twenty-one. The bonding of interests and goals and temperaments that began as one century ended and another began was to carry these two remarkable people forward on a passionate quest for beauty, fame, and financial security. In meeting, courting, and marrying Lucretia, Wallace made a watershed decision about his destiny that accounts for much of the triumph and tragedy of his short and passionate life.

However, the most wonderful and deeply rewarding part of his life lay many years ahead of him as the year 1900 drew to a close. In the December letter to Pops he refers with satisfaction to a visit, presumably to his famous father, by two artists he had come to know at the Academy. He had in fact studied under them quite recently. William Merritt Chase, who was later to found his own art school in New York and whose reputation today is among the foremost in American painting, was interested enough in Gilchrist to take the time, along with Cecelia Beaux, to visit the Gilchrists and inquire about Wallace's trip overseas. Of course the first questions Chase and Beaux would ask were, "Where is he living? What artist is he studying?" Chase may even have written Wallace following this meeting, because he says to Pops, "Hope to hear from him soon." Perhaps Chase's visit was a mere courtesy call, with an element of friendly pedagogical concern. On the other hand, how many of his students were treated to such a visit? Even after considering that the visit was as much a sign of respect for the musician as for the young painter, it is hard to shrug off the feeling that Chase and Beaux were recognizing in their genteel fashion the flowering of a major artistic talent.

The most delightful and revealing part of this letter, however, lies in the postscript, which contains some references to his brothers. He'd like to see "Chas. get up and travel," he says in the midst of his first trip to Europe, and the ironic thing about this bit of gratuitous advice to his older brother, who was already twenty-seven years old, is that by the time Charlie died in 1920, he was a world traveler who had logged more travel time than all the rest of his family combined, while his brother Wallace, after a second trip to Europe with his new bride in 1902-1904, became so busy with family and career that his travels were thereafter largely confined to the eastern seaboard of the United States.

Charlie, however, was never to marry and settle down. He led a romantic and fascinating life, and like their older sister, Anna, he cherished his freedom of action and managed somehow to be attractive to many women but close to only one for any length of time.

It was completely in character for Wallace to want to help his two brothers. They were athletic rivals, to be sure, but there was a deep bond of affection among the family members, of which this brief word of advice to Charlie was just one instance.

Finally, in the same postscript Wallace makes a half jesting remark about his little brother, who would outlive, outearn, and outspend all of his siblings in the course of a distinguished career as an architect. Teddy at this time is just three months shy of his sixteenth birthday as Wallace says to Pops that Charlie could "take Ted along perhaps, what good is school to Ted anyway? the little sinner—I think school holds back many a good fellow instead of pushing him ahead." Whether Teddy and Charlie do in fact travel together is not known, but Wallace now says something totally unrelated, in his by now habitual jumping from topic to topic to get in all his points before space runs out. He says that since Teddy has applied to a high school in Philadelphia (Drexel), he should have good lunches. "Hope if Ted gets into Drexel he'll manage to have better lunches than I did at the Manual—it's a dreadfully important matter."

Then comes the last line, so typical of his humor and chatty style of writing: "These breakfasts of bread and butter and coffee agree with me perfectly." The letter jumps from topic to topic, indicating his haste to finish so he can get on with his work, and the tremendous drive and restlessness in this ambitious young painter.

Fifteen days later it is New Year's Day, 1901. Wallace again sits with his pen and writes to Pops, this time at considerable length. He responds to what must have been some words of praise relayed to him from Cecelia Beaux, cautioning Pops to "make allowances for Miss Beaux's extravagances and especially after this coming through Mrs. Burnham." A statement like this again indicates his healthy capacity for cool, objective appraisal of his own work, showing his desire to discount all gushy and meaningless plaudits for the sake of truly knowing the worth of his art. Only with this approach could he ever hope to grow. Nevertheless, the news that a painting had sold

Sisters

www.meyersphoto.com

puts him in such "good spirits that I am afraid I made quite a fool of myself at the supper table tonight by getting into an hysterical fit of laughing." The painting in question was very likely done the preceding summer after his graduation from the Academy, and Wallace recalls having had a difficult time with the head, adding, "I know Mr. Chase could not have been pleased with it."

In this letter one begins to appreciate that Gilchrist is not only a talented painter but also a highly verbal man. In all of his letters, when he is not rushed, this skill emerges. Even so eminent a personage as Bowdoin's president Kenneth Sills remarks upon this when writing, a quarter century later, his letter of condolence to Lucretia: "When he was doing the wall portrait, I used genuinely to enjoy sitting for him—he always had so many ideas and was so intelligent not only about art but about things in general."

Considering that Wallace's maternal grandfather was a clergyman, and that his own father was as much if not more of a musical leader of people than a published composer of music, Wallace's verbal aptitude is no real surprise. It must have served him well as a portraitist, for one has only to imagine how difficult a time a painter of people's faces would have were he unable somehow to charm them along with words and wit.

In this New Year's Day letter Wallace also announces his decision to travel south, visiting Italy, which pleases Pops, and topping it off with Velásquez in Madrid. He also says there is small chance he will become a copyist, and that "some people I think are too much afraid of their individuality and won't learn from others." As he looks to the future he realizes how intensely he wants to make his studio a "tempting environ-

www.meyersphoto.com

www.meyersphoto.com

*The Gray Veil*                                   *Bess*

ment." He doesn't blame people who withdraw patronage from an artist who "shows such bad taste in his surroundings—it runs right into their work."

The letter ends with one of his most revealing comments. In talking of his upcoming journey to Italy and Spain he says that his "old love for nature only comes over me when I am with Lucretia, it is so in more ways than one, I need her to be myself."

Two days later, on Thursday, January 3, 1901, Wallace decides to write Pops another letter because, as he says, "For the last few days I have been thinking over my plans for the future and have managed to turn them completely upside down." Having lived in Haarlem for the last twelve weeks, he feels he has done more than enough copying for a while and "should like to do something." What he means is simply that all of Europe lies spread out at his feet, so to speak, and he wants to see it, especially its art treasures, while his money holds out. He is also ever so eager to get on with his career. "The chief thing I shall learn in all this experience is that a fellow is better off when settled quietly at home working in his own way than when roaming around the world in an unsettled state of mind with his heart aching like the devil morning noon and night."

Having said this he details his travel plans, as follows: he and Joe will tour southward by way of the German cities of Kessel, Leipzig, Dresden, and Munich, then go to Vienna and the "principal points of Italy." Finally he will go to Madrid to see and copy Velásquez, after which on to London and home to America.

In his next letter two weeks later, on January 17, he is about to set off the next day traveling third class through Germany by himself, a prospect he does not relish. Most of this letter concerns his slender budget and a photo he bought in Antwerp of a painting, almost certainly by Hals, which he calls "the most delicate, refined, and graceful piece of painting you ever saw." It is clear from these remarks and from his earlier comments about the virtues of American women that Wallace already has an exquisite sensitivity for the subject in which he will excel. Women, old and young, dressed and undressed, will be his forte, but only beautiful ones, for as his son once said, "Father used to get a little depressed when there were no beautiful women around for him to study, enjoy, and paint." Above all, to paint.

With this letter he finally sets his course for Madrid and the wonders of Velásquez. As for Madrid he says simply, "I don't know what will be the state of my mind. You see a fellow lays plans—and then he goes ahead and learns something—and that makes him think differently perhaps, and that changes his plans." Fourteen days later, February 1, 1901, he and Joe are in Vienna for two days, still traveling third class. He reports having been "a little sickish for a while" in Munich, "but pulled out of it all right with the use of hot scotch whiskey and such things. I feel pretty well now having left only the remains of a cough."

He is now more than ever convinced that America is the place for a painter to be. "The school life and studio life over here I could not stand for one week. I saw the Munich schools and they don't touch our Academy either in conveniences or the quality of work done there. I know the work done there. I know the work of most of the best German artists too but it doesn't amount to much. America is the country and I am coming back there soon. We don't half appreciate what we have." Then, although he says, "I'm sick of these foreigners," he also says, "Do you know there are some fifty or sixty Velásquezes waiting for me in Madrid if I can ever get there!"

Just over one week later he writes to Pops from Florence, where he gets wonderful news. His father has promised him $150. This elates him, for he has had the usual budget problems and had only $80 left before reaching Florence. It will cost him $50 just for the fare from Naples to Madrid. He plans to continue south from Florence to take in Rome for a few days, then go to Naples, where presumably he will find a ship bound for Spain and travel overland to Madrid. He and Joe have read in Baedeker's guidebook that Spain is "about the worst country in the face of the earth to travel through—I don't fancy it at all, it is bad enough here."

Italy is cold, snow has fallen in Florence during the night, and consequently "out of doors sketching is impracticable." He is glad to be seeing so much but feels unproductive, saying, "This idleness now makes me feel very uneasy." Nevertheless he hopes it will be warm enough in Spain for some outdoor work.

He responds to his father's description of the latest exhibition at the Pennsylvania Academy by saying, "I believe Philadelphia is quite the art center of America—Harry and Joe and I have decided to make it so anyhow. I hope they put through that scheme of building studio buildings in Philadelphia. Studios are frightfully expensive there." His final sentence is vintage Wallace: "Mr. Kaufman's remark about my portrait of you being better than anything in the exhibition is ridiculous." He cannot at his age conceive of himself as the equal of giants like Sargent or Chase or Whistler.

March finds Wallace safely in Madrid, but in his letter of March 13 we learn nothing about the supposedly miserable journey across Spain, and there is no mention of Rome or Naples either. A Mrs. Burnham had sent him some money, which enables him to go home by way of London instead of sailing directly from Gibraltar to New York.

In all likelihood this is the same Burnham family that is later close to brother Charles when he travels to the West to film himself scaling the coastal cliffs of California. In making this contribution, Mrs. Burnham perhaps becomes Wallace's first patroness. If so, it represents his first taste of patronage, which was never abundant in his life. Had it been there more often, it might have changed his life, career, and reputation.

As Wallace must by now have discovered, Velásquez was totally unlike Hals in that he received, when he was just a year older than Wallace, the sort

McKeen Street dining room

of patronage most painters can only dream of. He was appointed court painter to King Philip IV of Spain, yet his work suffered no more from this good fortune than Hals's did from adversity. The Dutchman was never able to make a decent living, was forever being sued for nonpayment of debts, and died a poor man. Both men were among the greatest painters in human history, but while they lived they were just as subject to the whims of fate as anyone else.

Wallace in Madrid is a repeat performance of Wallace in Haarlem. There is nothing too wonderful he can say about Velásquez, and he vows that if he had another two or three months to spend, he would spend it in Madrid. He reports that many painters he knows who spent years in Paris and London were sorry they hadn't gone first to Madrid. In this regard it is noteworthy that between 1880 and 1920 Velásquez's reputation reached a high it had never touched before, even though he had lived and died over two and a half centuries before Wallace was born. It is sheer coincidence that Wallace finds himself in the very place where Velásquez worked at the very time his fame reached its zenith.

"I am copying Velásquez morning and afternoon from 9 to 4," he writes, "and if a month of that does me no good it is my own fault. I may have half a dozen or so copies to bring away from here and I have more in my trunk in Haarlem." Approximately eight years after writing these words from Spain, Wallace writes to a New York artist named Charles Rosen in connection with his application for membership in the Salmagundi Club. In this letter he also wishes Rosen a wonderful trip to Europe and urges him to visit Madrid. He then makes the following statement: "Madrid is in my mind the hub of the world—the centre and the Mecca of the Art World—Our Holy Grail lies there."

In London, finally, Wallace writes on March 30 that he likes the city and the life there, but the months away from Lucretia and his family and the cultural milieu of life in Philadelphia are beginning to tell on his nerves. In an unusual statement for him he

*The Gilchrist Family at Breakfast*

www.meyersphoto.com

confides to Pops that "I sometimes have turmoils inside me that give me no rest for spaces of five or six consecutive days." This comes from a man who six months earlier was speculating about staying abroad for a year or more! It is typical of Wallace always to expect more than his nerves and stamina can sustain, but that sort of optimism was very much in line with the zeitgeist of the day. In 1901, however, his pain was purely personal, a young man nearly lovesick, increasingly homesick, always impatient to move on with his life, and now about to return to his darling Lucretia.

On April 2 we find him on the Isle of Wight at a place called Tushwater. He has come here hoping to sketch out of doors, but the weather is poor, and after Madrid the English Channel in March must have felt bitterly uncomfortable. In any case, he is now so homesick and lonesome that he really cannot work well at all. He almost seems to be shouting his frustration as he writes, "How could I in this state of mind (or rather state of heart) come to this quiet, beautiful, lonesome little spot, live here for a month or so and do sane work—not for a minute. I couldn't stand it for more than two days and I am going back tomorrow."

*At Her Writing Desk*

The only place for Wallace now is Philadelphia. He sums it up like this: "I came to Haarlem with a purpose, to Italy with a purpose, to Madrid with a purpose, to London indifferently (at the injunction of others) and I am going home with a purpose." There is perhaps something close to anger in his tone, as if to tell the family that only he knows what is best for his life, his career, and his future. "There is a clock ticking behind me," he says. "Each minute is a gun. Each new one opens a new possibility for the life, and each one lost of that life seems to be like a murdered one."

Sitting in London, visiting a few of the people his father may have known, stopping at a showing of someone's work which he has to pretend to like, he is really just marking time until the ship leaves for America. He recalls some of the things that happened in Europe, remembers how thoroughly sick he got at having to bargain for everything he bought in Spain. He says he hates modern day Spain, Italy, and France. Only glimpses of their bygone glories redeem those lands in his mind. German militarism he finds despicable. Though the Spanish were "better than we thought and much nicer than the Italians," and though the German ballet had a "certain clean cut refinement and daintiness about it that I need in my work," Wallace seems hardly able to enjoy these last few days before the North German Lloyd luxury liner *Kaiser Wilhelm der Grosse* carries him off to America on the seventeenth of April, 1901.

As a first trip abroad his was a truly difficult, exhausting, but immensely moving and influential one. The impressions he received would stay with him all his life, and the training he put himself through would prove to be the wisest possible use of his time, for Hals and Velásquez have few peers in the painting of portraits. But now America beckoned, and Lucretia.

When Wallace finished his travels in the early spring of 1901, he discovered that he had just enough money left to book passage in steerage. Despite the advent of the great luxury liners, any voyage across the North Atlantic in 1901 could be an intimidating experience in which passengers discovered that a day or so of rough weather could turn the romance into unrelieved misery. Since Wallace was already touchy about his health, he must have had some moments of real fear as he boarded the *Kaiser Wilhelm* on April 17 and climbed down the long, steep steel steps deeper and deeper into the ship until he reached steerage, much of it below the waterline, where he would live for the next week or so.

Years later, as he recounted the adventure to young Bill, he vividly recalled huddling among the immigrants and the poor, listening to the sickening thump of the huge propellers as they lifted clear out of the churning waters of a rough sea. He remembered watching miserably as the green of the undersea waters streamed past the dim portholes, and he told of watching a fellow passenger, who obviously had a cast-iron stomach, consume a raw fish with much belly rubbing gusto. Needless to say, he was seasick most of the way to New York.

By early May 1901, Gilchrist had returned to Philadelphia and was sufficiently recovered from the ordeal of his Atlantic crossing to begin contemplating his next step. A joyful reunion with Lucretia led to the making of a wedding date, and on January 1, 1902, Lucretia's twenty-second birthday, they were married in Bethlehem, Pennsylvania. A local paper ran the following notice:

Bethlehem, Jan. 1 (Special)—In the Moravian Church, at 3 o'clock this afternoon, Miss Lucretia Mott deSchweinitz and William Wallace Gilchrist, Jr., of Philadelphia, were married in the presence of guests from New York, Steelton, Mechanicsburg, Philadelphia, and other places. The cousin of the bride, Rev. Paul deSchweinitz, secretary of the governing board of the American Moravian Church, officiated. The bride, on her mother's side, is a great granddaughter of Lucretia Mott, the noted Quaker preacher in abolition days, and on her father's side is a granddaughter of the late Bishop Edmund deSchweinitz, a noted Moravian divine. Mr. and Mrs. Gilchrist will live in Germantown.

Three weeks later, at the Pennsylvania Academy's big annual exhibition in Philadelphia, Gilchrist, who would turn twenty-three on March 2, joined the ranks of exhibiting artists for the first time. His single entry was a portrait of his father's good friend and fellow musician Phillip Goepp. It was the only work he would submit until 1905, because he and Lucretia had decided to undertake a second trip to Europe, for an indefinite stay, before settling down in one place to begin a family.

There were both personal and professional reasons for this decision. Foremost among them was the fact that Lucretia had never been abroad, had never seen the paintings of Franz Hals and all the other artistic wonders of Europe. Then, too, it was only natural for a pair as young as Lucretia and Wallace to take the fullest possible advantage of their brief period of freedom. They knew that once they had children, this sort of freedom might never be theirs again.

However, the professional reason for another trip was even more compelling than the personal one. According to Bill, his father had heard that the German painters were perfecting a new and better technique for painting the human eye. Having chosen to specialize in portraiture, Wallace really had no choice but to investigate. To appreciate how well he mastered this critical skill, one has only to look at the portrait he titled *Uncle John*.

Although the newlyweds were away from as late as the fall of 1902, and possibly several months longer, not a single piece of corre-

*Field and Woods in Mist*

www.meyersphoto.com

spondence has been found that could throw light on what they did, thought, learned, or experienced. If they wrote or kept a diary, the documents are either lost or destroyed. It seems likely that they wrote chatty, infrequent letters to the family, not the sort one would keep in a scrapbook. Lucretia was careful of what she left lying about, inclined to be secretive about anything intimate or private. She would have been careful of what she wrote, and being naturally frugal she would have economized by sending as few letters as possible across the Atlantic.

Fortunately a few key pieces of information do exist, all in two short letters and on one page of a family scrapbook, where Lucretia pasted three photographs taken by a friend of Harry Rittenberg, Wallace's traveling companion in 1900. They show the interior of what appears to be a large studio with two chairs, a writing table, a bed or couch, and several large paintings. In two of the photos Wallace is posed with his palette and brush, once by a large painting on an easel, the other sitting in a rocking chair working on something he holds. Perhaps he is mixing paints. The room is shown from several angles and is fitted with floor-to-ceiling drapes to create what might have been a private sleeping area. At the bottom of the page, in Lucretia's hand, is written, "80 Georgas Strasse Muenchen Nov. 1902–Mai 1903."

Their first winter in Europe, therefore, we may assume they spent in Munich, Germany. In the spring of 1903, probably by early June, Lucretia must have discovered she was pregnant. Between the birth of their first child the following February 3 in London and their last days in the Munich apartment, only a few words written by Lucretia on the back of a photograph hint at their whereabouts. The photo is of a painting called *Baroness*, on the back of which Lucretia has penciled the words:

*After Breakfast*

"Baroness–Haarlem–Holland 1903." Wallace must have taken his wife to the same town in Holland where, two and a half years earlier, he had copied and studied Franz Hals's great work.

How long they remained in Holland is unknown. What other stops or side trips they made between Munich and London is also unknown. What is certain is that in London, on February 3, 1904, Lucretia and Wallace became the parents of a baby girl they named Margaret and called Peggy. Since travel in winter was difficult and unappealing, and because their resources were quite limited, and not least of all because their numbers were about to increase in February, we can assume that they settled down to live somewhere in London in the fall of 1903.

Wallace had already made a few contacts in London on his earlier trip in late March and early April of 1901. In a letter to his father dated March 30, 1901, from Ludgate Circus, he writes: "I like London, and I like the life here and everything. If Lucretia were here I would not concern myself much about my next step but settle down here for a while." Now that he and his expectant wife were in London, he would have been impatient to begin painting and above all to obtain some commission work so their stay could be prolonged.

*Daydreams*

www.meyersphoto.com

By the following spring, however, Wallace was searching for some supplemental income. We know this from two short letters found in the Pennsylvania Academy's archives. In the first one, dated May 8, 1904, when Peggy was three months old, Wallace's father writes to an Academy official named Harrison S. Morris asking whether he could help advertise some English classes Wallace planned to give so they could remain longer in London. In his father's words, "He is anxious to remain on the other side to gain some position before returning, and as a help the scheme suggested by the enclosed has occurred to him." Two days later Mr. Morris graciously responded, saying they would do "anything in our power to promote" the English classes. Wallace may or may not have made some money from this scheme, but the mere fact that he considered it implies that he could not earn enough from painting to enable them to remain in London. In the heart of what was then the mighty British Empire, Gilchrist in 1904 was but a small American fish in a very large British lake.

Between May of 1904 and January of 1905 is another undocumented period. On January 23, 1905, the Pennsylvania Academy opened its one-hundredth annual exhibition, and Wallace submitted three works, which were on display until March 4, two days after his twenty-sixth birthday. The three were called *Portrait of Helen J. Sellers*,

*W. W. Gilchrist, Music Director,* and *Grandfather's Prints.* There is no proof that these were painted in Philadelphia during the summer, fall, and winter of 1904, but it does seem very unlikely that he would have painted them all before his second trip abroad without also submitting them to the show held in 1902.

Directories kept by the Germantown Historical Society show his address from 1901 to 1904 as 5914 Wayne Avenue, indicating that between his two trips to Europe and following his return with wife and child sometime in early 1904, he and Lucretia lived with his parents, probably with Anna, then thirty-three and single, Teddy, who was then nineteen, and possibly Charlie, who was thirty-one. The house was large enough for all of them, and with the help of Anna and Wallace's mother, who was fifty-seven, Lucretia would have had more than enough help with the baby. Multigenerational households were more the rule than the exception in those days. The huge old homes still found in villages, towns, and cities all over America attest to this important sociological fact. Today, much of the economic and spiritual malaise bemoaned by commentators and scholars comes from the separation of the generations. There are enormous economic benefits as well as feelings of warmth and security that disappear when the older and younger generations live apart.

The old directories do not list Gilchrist for 1905, but beginning in 1906 and running straight through until 1915, when they moved to Maine, the family lived in West Philadelphia at 129 South 46th Street. This placed them about sixteen blocks west of the Schuylkill River, slightly beyond the University of Pennsylvania, where his father had received his degree in music and where Charlie had his degree in civil engineering. This section of the city, though perhaps not as fashionable as the Germantown or Chestnut Hill neighborhoods north of the city, was nevertheless very convenient by trolley to Gilchrist's studio at 716 Locust Street, near Washington Square.

In 1907 the senior Gilchrists decided that after eighteen years on Wayne Avenue, and with their four children all out on their own, it was time to move to smaller, more manageable quarters. Since they now had two granddaughters living in West Philadelphia, Nelly having been born the preceding August, they chose an address on Spruce Street a short walk from Wallace and Lucretia. From 1907 until 1912 the musician and his wife lived here and became grandparents again in 1910 when Bill was born.

In the summer of 1906 Anna was traveling in Europe when Lucretia gave birth to Nelly, on August 16. Wallace wrote to his sister from Montrose, Pennsylvania, where Lucretia had spent her earliest years before her father sold his dairy business and moved his family down to Bethlehem:

Dear Anna,
Here it is the 31st of August and you have not heard about your little niece born over two weeks ago! She came too late for us to send you a letter to Liverpool and we did not quite see the use in going to the expense of a cablegram. She was born at 4:15 p.m. Thursday, August 16 and came into the world in quite the proper way—just as Peggy did and without causing her mother any abnormal discomfiture or complications. Just at this minute she is calling lustily for her meal. Peggy takes to her very naturally. Calls her "baby sister," pats her gently and says "Isn't it cunning," etc. etc. etc. It would be simply impossible to tell you

all she does say—for she simply talks right straight ahead now and says nearly anything she wants to. Charles came up for our Sunday last week, and as soon as Peggy saw him she said "Pitty soon Nanna come"—so you see she remembers you. I tell her stories in bed every morning and she always wants to hear the one about you. You ought to see her now—she is blossoming out more each day and is certainly a picture of perfect childhood. The little sister is to be named Ellen Lord.

Your letters have grown more interesting as your trip progressed, and the last, from Heidelburg was quite a corker. —You have seen some of the real life this time and no doubt about it. I have followed you all through with envy, and could see in my memory a great many of the places you visited. It must have been fine to have had such a jolly crowd, and I can hardly wait to hear more of the details.

Affec. Wallace.

I suppose there is no use asking you to come see us even for a day for you will of course go right to Suttons. Take good care of Mads and see that Pops has plenty of recreation.

In the fall of 1906 Gilchrist, who with Nelly's arrival now had three dependents, decided to supplement his income and broaden his reputation in Philadelphia by teaching portraiture. At that time The Philadelphia School of Design for Women was the "oldest and largest institution of its kind in the United States." Then located at Broad and Masters and today at the Parkway at Twentieth and called the Moore College of Art, it was founded in 1844 by Mrs. Sarah Peter, wife of the British consul at Philadelphia. Gilchrist was engaged by the school to teach portraiture from both life and antique. He was scheduled for several hours on Mondays and Tuesdays throughout the academic year, which began on October 1, 1906, and finished May 29, 1907.

As a result of this teaching, he made contact with the principal, Emily Sartain, and probably with all or most of the six other teachers who served that year: Elliott Daingerfield, Samuel Murray, Henry Snell, Florence Einstein, Harriet Sartain, and Miss Moore. In the spring of 1907, between April 12 and 20, Gilchrist arranged a large show of his own work in the school's galleries. There were some thirty-five paintings, including three copies of Hals and Velásquez.

One of the benefits of any successful show is the chance to meet likely buyers, especially the women who would offer to serve as "hostesses." In an age when many women did not feel constrained to seek gainful employment, whether for money or prestige or self-fulfillment, Lucretia would consult with friends and family to assemble a group of socially prominent women who were delighted to be asked to serve refreshments and make visitors feel welcome. Thus Gilchrist benefited greatly from the contacts established over the years by both the Gilchrist generations.

He also benefited from his New York connections, which grew quite naturally from the fact that his grandfather, the man who as a small boy had moved from Montreal down to New York and later married his childhood friend Redelia Cox, spent most of his life in metropolitan New York. The Cox family included Jacob D. Cox, a scholarly man who distinguished himself first as a major general in the Union army, then as governor of Ohio, and finally as secretary of the interior under President Grant. One of General Cox's sons was a New York artist named Kenyon Cox.

www.meyersphoto.com

*Congress Square*                                     Portland Museum of Art

At some point in the early spring of 1907, Wallace must have written to Kenyon Cox, who was his great-uncle, to ask if he could rent the artist's New York studio for a commission he might have that summer. A piece of Cox's reply has survived, in which he offers the studio for $7.50 a week and goes on to offer Wallace some words of praise and suggestions for improvement. The following excerpt shows how naturally a painter's work transcends the bounds of geography. It is also an early indication that Gilchrist's reputation had already leaped beyond the limits of Philadelphia to the great throbbing metropolis just ninety miles northeast, which Philadelphians half admire and half loathe.

I must say what I have several times been on the verge of writing especially to tell you, how much I, and many others on the jury, liked your two pictures at the Academy this spring. *The Portrait of Mrs. Parrish* [probably the wife of Maxfield Parrish] was especially delightful in tone and arrangement and I greatly regretted that you had not entered it for one of the prizes. I had it on my list of pictures to vote for, and I think it might have had a fair show for something. And now I am going to take the privilege of an older, and perhaps more

*After the Storm*

www.meyersphoto.com

old-fashioned, artist to express my regret at a certain negligence of drawing, particularly in the extremities, which I think the most serious defect of your charming work. I do not ask for definite edges of hard execution, but I cannot think a more expressive rendering of the form and structure of arms and hands would interfere with the quality of your painting, any more than it does with Hals or Velásquez, who were not only painters but infallible draughtsmen as well.

I should not make this criticism if I did not like your work. I want you to be still more of a credit to the family than you already are! I think your other qualities safe to develop of themselves and that you may safely put a good deal of effort, for a time at least, into achieving a more secure mastery of form.

I hope when you are next in New York in the winter you will look us up, as both my wife and I are desirous of knowing you. Give my best love to your father, whom I am sorry to see so little of.

During these years Gilchrist, in addition to dealing with well-intentioned criticism, renting a studio in New York, being a father to two little girls, and painting commissions, also found time to propose a cooperative gallery owned by local artists and run by a Mr. White. In two letters to John E. Trask, who was managing director of the Pennsylvania Academy from 1905 to 1912, Gilchrist elaborates on his idea, writing in the first letter just before Thanksgiving in 1909:

> The affair is what might be called an informal gallery or art shop. It occupies part of the first floor of the building at 716 Locust Street [where Gilchrist had his studio]. One will have to ring the bell for admission, the passer-by will be little concerned, and we expect only those who are especially interested to patronize it. A number of my friends such as Borie, Tyson, Pearson, Garber, and others are interested in an advisory way. Thus it is a gallery managed chiefly by artists, run for the sake of artists, and managed by Mr. White on the business end. We depend on our friends to speak a good word for us—and some have helped considerably in securing pictures. Mr. Hale has very kindly spoken to some of the Boston men who are going to send—and through Pearson—Weir and several others have promised to contribute.

Two days later, November 19, 1909, Wallace writes again to Trask:

> Mr. White's gallery is in fact S. S. White trading for White's Gallery. The financial responsibility rests entirely upon Mr. White alone. I hope this explains matters fully—I had thought that I had made it clear, but it is clearer still that my understanding of business matters, and my vocabulary of terms relative thereto is as slight as possible. I am glad you are in sympathy with the movement and only hope we can make a success of it.

Apparently Gilchrist in these early years tried more than one novel approach to collaboration with his contemporaries, as the following letter from Maxfield Parrish indicates. The so-called "mahogany deal" is a mystery:

> December 14, 1908
> Windsor, Vermont
> My dear Gilchrist:
> I wish I could go in with you on the ground floor of the mahogany deal, but alas I cannot. The wood excites me unduly, and the doctor has forbidden me to have it around. As to Hoag, I shall never speak to him again.
> With best wishes,
> Maxfield Parrish

Gilchrist also wrote a letter to the *Philadelphia Ledger*. It was published on February 5, 1909, and is the only one of its kind in the family papers.:

> As an artist I should like to express the pleasure I have taken in your editorial on "The American Artist," appearing in this morning's paper. It seems to me to express the situation more aptly than anything I have read for some time. I would venture to say that the present exhibition at the Pennsylvania Academy of

the Fine Arts shows a higher standard of work than the general public or even the usual buyers themselves begin to realize. What the American artist has accomplished in the face of discouragement is really astonishing—and what he might accomplish with even a tenth of the patronage that artists were accustomed to during the ages of the Medici and others we read of can only be dreamed.

In 1913 Gilchrist moved his studio to 904 Walnut Street, a few blocks closer to City Hall. This move appears to mark the start of a gradual transition from Philadelphia to Maine via New York City.* In 1914 he gave his studio address as West 40th Street in New York City, and on February 26, 1915, he took legal possession of the old farmhouse in Harpswell, Maine, where he moved with the family that summer.

He had already gained a foothold in New York in 1909 by joining the prestigious Salmagundi Club at 47 Fifth Avenue. He must have garnered a goodly amount of commission work during those years, because his studio address in both 1916 and 1917 was given in the Academy's exhibition catalogue as 146 West 55th Street. Letters also refer to Bryant Park Studios (in early 1914) and to the Carnegie Studios. The first letter to the William Macbeth Gallery at 450 Fifth Avenue is dated December 27, 1912, and earlier that month Gilchrist painted a commission for the *New York Times* called *Christmas Shopping*, which appeared in a special Christmas issue on Sunday, December 8, 1912.

Having done well as an instructor in Philadelphia following Nelly's birth in 1906, Gilchrist undertook a similar engagement in New York at the Art Students League beginning in October 1910, when Billy was just a month old. By coincidence, he taught in the same faculty that year with William Merritt Chase, who was some thirty years older than Gilchrist and had taught him at the Academy over a decade earlier. Both artists taught portraiture, but Gilchrist earned only $75 a month while Chase, who was sixty-one and far better known, drew a salary of $125 a month.

Chase, for whom Gilchrist had a very high regard, had a most unfortunate experience while teaching at his own school in New York. He had accepted a student named Mrs. O'Brien, who became so exceedingly troublesome for him that he finally asked her to leave, whereupon her husband came to the school, asked for Mr. Chase, went into his classroom, and proceeded to assault Chase rather brutally. He knocked him to the floor, dragged him by his collar to the studio where his wife was painting, and demanded an apology in her presence. Chase was laid up for some time and later sued O'Brien, who in court mumbled an insincere apology. Chase resigned from his school and six months later, hearing of O'Brien's death from pneumonia, shouted, "Him! I hope he's in hell—where he belongs."

*In October of 1916 a young woman who was engaged to marry Lucretia's brother George drove with her fiancé from New Jersey up to Roadside to visit with Lucretia and the children. On the way north they had dinner in a town on the Connecticut coast. There she met Wallace, who was probably painting a commission, and she recalls that "afterward he danced with me. He was a beautiful dancer." In 1916 tea dances at the New York hotels were very popular, and Wallace, she writes, "was quite well known for dancing the new and fashionable tango."

*Something of Interest*

www.meyersphoto.com

*Kneeling to Mend*

www.meyersphoto.com

## GILCHRIST AND THE ART WORLD

Gilchrist's feeling for the art world was probably ambivalent. Many of the best-known artists of his day were his personal friends, acquaintances and teachers, especially those such as Chase, Garber, Redfield, Homer, and Beaux, who lived in or near Philadelphia or Brunswick, Maine. He contributed almost every year to the Pennsylvania Academy's spring exhibition, was now and then asked to help jury them, belonged to several of the best-known painters' clubs in Philadelphia and New York, and was a much-liked teacher at the Art Students League and at Pittsburgh's Carnegie Institute, among other places. He also dealt with dealers such as New York's Macbeth Galleries, letters to and from whom are available at the Smithsonian's New York City branch.

He certainly cannot have felt any strong need to rebel against an established Salon, as did the great Frenchman Manet, and as did the so-called Ten American Painters. In fact, by the time Gilchrist began his career in 1900 there was not much left to rebel against. The Bastille had already been breached by those preceding him, and he himself adopted toward the next art revolution a strongly negative attitude, which might explain his remark about the French gallery at the Paris exposition of 1900: France, he wrote to his father, had "acres of the darndest trash you ever saw."

Yet he also never really had any special affection for the dealers. Though he was unfailingly correct in his correspondence, in several of the brief notes to Macbeth one senses a tightly controlled edginess verging on contempt for the mentality of the dealer, and in private he vented considerable anger and frustration at the mercenary attitude of mere businessmen whose dull view of life he found depressing.

www.meyersphoto.com

*Girl Sewing*

His own in-laws were often highly critical of Wallace's supposed failure to support Lucretia and the children in a more comfortable style. His feelings were stung by this, and he would sometimes react with a sharp tongue very different from the usual happy and rather sweet serenity for which he was better known among friends and family. As far as he was concerned, his function in life was to create the most beautiful paintings he could possibly squeeze from his short lifetime. The somewhat mean-spirited attitude of his in-laws merely emphasized that his work was of an excellence that some people could not value perceptively. He knew only too well and at great personal cost that most painters must trust to posterity and struggle to create work that another generation will admire and love.

Until he found one or two wealthy patrons willing to help him and his family survive, he was forced to spend most of his creative energies on portraiture, yet even here the time was well and wisely spent, beginning with his decision to visit Europe to learn from Hals and Velásquez, and continuing with a second decision made early in 1901, in response to a suggestion from his father, to reject the field of landscape painting as his specialty, using it more as a relief from the intense indoor concentration on portraiture and the New England interiors that are now considered among his best work.

While Wallace never enjoyed a reliable income from any patron, he did occasionally receive important gifts of money from friends and family members. In a letter Wallace wrote from Madrid on March 13, 1901, he remarks to Pops: "You are probably just at this moment getting my letter telling you that I am coming home on the 31st. I don't know what you think of this. But now since your letters and Mrs. Burnham's money, I have decided to change and go to London on the way home."

A struggling young artist must use whatever family connections he has, and Wallace was more fortunate than most in this regard. His famous father was known to precisely the sort of people who normally constitute the clientele of an artist, and when Wallace went about setting up a studio in the spring of 1901, he would have been keenly aware of the importance of his father's reputation as an assist to his career. Today, in the perspective gained from the years since his death, it appears that Wallace and his father may have approximately equal stature in the world of fine arts, but when the artist returned from Europe in April of 1901, he desperately needed whatever social and professional connections he could find. Perhaps, too, there is something unique about the way things work in Philadelphia. Bill thought so, telling everyone that whereas in Boston what counts is how much you know and in New York it is how much you have, in Philadelphia it's who you know that counts.

Ambivalent as Gilchrist may have been toward the art world, the critics who reviewed his shows were decidedly unambivalent in their praise. It is not difficult to read between the lines of newspaper articles which, over several decades, brought descriptions of his paintings to the public at large, first in Philadelphia and later in Maine. Those that give only cursory attention were done by people not well versed in painting, whereas the majority show real insight into the strengths of a particular work. To be fortunate in one's critics is not the least good luck a painter may hope for.

As early as 1909, Gilchrist began to be noticed for his skill in painting women. On December 20 of that year, the Art Club of Philadelphia opened a show of some forty paintings by twenty-one well-known artists. Participants included Chase, Hassam, Homer, Redfield, Tarbell, Weir, Garber, and deCamp. Gilchrist submitted three works, one of which he entitled *The Velvet Gown*. The newspaper critic who reviewed the show describes this painting as "certainly one of the two or three very best pictures in the room." He continues with the following: "The pose is unstudied and ingenuous, the expression of the features naive and winsome, and the coiffure, the folds of the gown, the curves of the throat and profile, the hands, are rendered with the unfaltering touch of the artist and not the mere technician."

A year later, the Art Club presented another show. The title was changed from Special Exhibition of Modern American Painters to Second Special Exhibition of Eminent Living American Painters, and the number of participants was almost doubled, each painter now being limited to just one entry. This time Gilchrist distinguished himself with *Lady Lynx*, which was purchased by the Club. On January 1, 1911, the *Philadelphia Public Ledger* published an 8 1/2 x 11 1/2" photograph of this painting, a signal honor for a painter at the start of his career.

The Art Club of Philadelphia, founded in 1874, was open not only to painters, but also to musicians, sculptors, and architects. The Club's 1912 annual report lists eighty-four "artist members," exactly 75% of whom were painters. Gilchrist, having been elected to membership in 1907, served on the twelve-man executive board in 1910. By 1912 he was on the Committee on Exhibitions and the Committee on Purchase of Works of Art.

John H. McFadden, who presided over the club's Board of Directors, reported significant growth in 1912, pointing out that membership had increased during the year from 852 to 883 men, of whom only eighty-four were actually artists. Fully 735 men, of whom 131 were classified "non-resident," paid the entrance fee of $100 and annual dues of $100. Artists were required to pay only $50.

The building that housed the club must have been a large and well-furnished one, for on the club's 1912 balance sheet, the building with all its furnishings and improvements was valued at $448,000.

Inside the club a visitor would find a ladies café, a ladies restaurant, and a ladies reception room where members' wives and children could congregate. In keeping with the mores of that day, however, the club was still very much a male preserve, and the men enjoyed access to a library with nearly 7,000 volumes, private rooms, bedrooms (where no card playing was allowed), a banquet room, the Red Room for luncheons and dinners, an exhibition gallery, a card room, and a billiards room. By the time Gilchrist relocated to Maine, he was rather proficient at billiards, and one can assume that much of this proficiency came from practice at the tables of this old Philadelphia institution, where he was a resident member for eight years.

The year 1910 was an eventful one for Gilchrist. On September 1 of that year he became the father of a baby boy. Little Billy, who would carry on the name of his Scottish ancestors, surprised everyone and

Photographic study for *Nelly in the Woods*

inconvenienced his mother by arriving on Cliff Island while the family vacationed. For a child who would one day grow up to design a light-weight rowboat, Cliff Island was a fitting place to begin. When the family moved to Maine in 1915, Billy was five years old and consequently grew up as more of a Mainer than a Philadelphian.

No one knows for certain just when in 1910 Gilchrist completed his now-famous *Girl in Pink*, but it makes sense to think that he could never have withheld anything so beautiful from public view for more than a few months. He probably had in mind to finish it for the Pennsylvania Academy's annual exhibition. That is where it first appeared in public, on February 5, 1911, when the Academy opened its doors for the great annual show of painting and sculpture.

From the beginning, the painting was a winner. Called *Portrait of Miss M*, it was one of five entries selected to be photographed for the catalogue. Academy exhibitions were very large, and the artists who contributed were among the best known in the nation. In 1923, for instance, 377 artists entered 565 paintings and sculptures; by 1930 there were 714 works of art. Therefore, even a painting as fine as *Girl in Pink* could not attain more than moderate distinction.

*The Artist's Daughter, Nelly,*
private collection, photo courtesy
H. V. Allison & Co., Inc.
Larchmont, NY

www.meyersphoto.com

*Nelly in the Studio*

As the years went by, however, this masterpiece gained increasing fame, winning a prize in San Francisco at the 1915 Panama-Pacific Exposition held to celebrate the opening of the Panama Canal. The painting was used for a picture postcard on which the title was changed to *Girl in Pink*.

For several years in the late 1980s and early 1990s, the painting hung in the third-floor gallery of the Portland Museum of Art, and few visitors could have realized how close this marvelous work came to being lost forever. In the incomplete but still useful listing by Gilchrist's older sister Anna, the painting is called *Pink Lady*, and under the Remarks column is the word "destroyed." Evidently when the painting was shipped

www.meyersphoto.com

*The Liberty Scarf*

back to Maine Gilchrist needed the frame. He removed the canvas and, finding himself short of space, simply rolled it up and set it aside.

There it remained, pushed off into a dark corner of an unheated room that once served as the hayloft for a small dairy farm. For nearly seventy years it lay in obscurity until one day, quite by accident, an art historian named William Barry stopped in Brunswick to give a talk at the Curtis Library. Afterward he spotted an unusual painting on the landing of the old stairwell and asked who the painter was. He was told about the Gilchrists, drove down the Cundy's Harbor Road, and was shown the old studio by Bill and his wife Bette. When he saw the painting, or what remained of it, he knew he'd found a masterpiece in desperate need of restoration. The painting was bought by Barridoff Galleries, restored, sold to a wealthy collector, and presented as a gift to the Portland Museum of Art, where for a long time it caused endless wonderment, especially to the wide eyes of school children, who marveled that any woman could dress so enchantingly.*

When Gilchrist completed *Girl in Pink*, probably late in 1910, he was thirty-one years old. In early 1911 he participated for the third time in the Art Club's annual spring show and again outdid himself by winning the Club's gold medal for a work he called *In the Music Room*. The critic who did the review called it: "a charming interior study, painted with the rich, warm, dusky color scheme this artist employs so well." He finished by saying that "there is at this time no American painter who surpasses him in respect to solid values of interior atmosphere, refined composition and imposing, dignified quality." In a sense, these words are the reward for seven years of struggle to get established.

In addition to club memberships and exhibitions, another way for a young and ambitious painter like Gilchrist to advance his name was to serve on a jury. This group of artists decides which works receive the prizes normally given out by the prestigious annual shows, some of them substantial amounts of money and all of them much sought-after. In May 1907, Gilchrist got a formal letter from the Pennsylvania Academy offering him a position on their jury for the winter show in 1908, and of course he accepted. What young artist would turn down a chance to have his name printed in the catalogue and to help decide who gets the prizes? It was an honor he readily accepted, along with Thomas Anshutz, Philip Hale, Ernest Lawson, and Willard Metcalf. It has to be assumed that his selection was due not only to his work as an artist but also to his talent for making himself personally attractive, and perhaps even to his famous father. Philadelphia is a very social town, and Gilchrist had all the opportunities he needed to develop the right connections. Underlying the politicking, of course, were his hard work and increasing success as an artist.

During the first two weeks of November 1909, the McClees Galleries on Walnut Street in Philadelphia staged a one-man show of thirty-two of Gilchrist's paintings. Scrapbook notes reveal that at least two were sold, one of them, *The Velvet Gown*, bringing $350. Knowing that a factory worker could earn $480 a year in Brunswick in 1915, one can assume that six years earlier in Philadelphia $350 was enough for one person to live on for close to one year. In today's dollars this sale might be equivalent to $6,000. Such is the high-stakes nature of the artist's life. Two months later the buyer of *The Velvet Gown*, a Mr. Fritz, must have been delighted to find his artistic judgment corroborated by the Philadelphia critics.

In the 107-year history of the Gilchrist men, the musician and his three sons, few months were so full of triumph and achievement as April 1907. The artist's older brother Charles, then thirty-three years old, was again recognized for his truly heroic conquest of Mexico's most dangerous mountain, Ixtacihuatl, a 17,000-foot peak seldom attempted, even by seasoned mountaineers. All during March the newspapers in Cuba, Mexico, and the United States had run illustrated accounts of his struggle, including pictures he took of a higher but easier peak, Popocatapetl, whose 18,000 feet he had scaled in a blinding snowstorm on the same trip to Mexico. On April 1, the *Philadelphia Press* did a long article, complete with Charlie's own photographs, detailing his four grueling attempts over eleven days to reach the summit, plagued by the nausea of mountain sickness, which stopped only when he tried fasting before his last triumphant sortie.

A year to the day after this article was run, Charles was invited to present an illustrated talk, which he called "Climbs on the Mexican Snow Mountains," to the Geographic Society of Philadelphia. He is reported to have said that nothing he had experienced in the Alps had prepared him for the danger and the grandeur of the great Mexican peaks. He was considered the first American to have reached the summit of Ixtacihuatl.

A few days later, in a vastly different arena of work and struggle, Friday, April 12, 1907, marked the opening of Wallace's first major one-man show at the Philadelphia School of Design for Women. The show was well received by all the reviewers, several newspapers printing large photographs of four of the thirty-five paintings: *Portrait of Dr. W. W. Gilchrist*, *The Yellow Chrysanthemum* (a woman in a long gown), *Spanish Dancing Girl*, (following, as many painters did, the huge success of Sargent's painting of Carmencita) and *Portrait of Miss Priscilla Poor*, in which can be seen the exquisite taste and sweetness of Gilchrist's portraits of children.

The one nude in the show elicited three quite different critical responses. One person said the full-length figure was handled with "skill and an eye for vivid color, marred by some rather crude whites in the drapery." Another wrote that the flesh tones were "in competition with the heavy pink of surrounding hangings, the former pallidly dominant even in defeat." Yet a third critic felt the nude was "painted in a bold, dashing manner" and was "an interesting study of form and flesh painting." Since the newspaper chose not to print a photograph of this nude, the reactions cannot be verified or understood, and once again we see how difficult it is to know what exactly the critics are talking about. One can only say that art critics often feel constrained to couch negative remarks within positive ones, so as not to discourage the painter or repel their readers.

*Grandma Sewing at Roadside*

www.meyersphoto.com

This particular show, coming as it did early in Gilchrist's career, encompassed work dating all the way back to his days as a student at the Academy and drew upon his studies in Europe. In particular, a painting entitled *Westminster Abbey by Night* was singled out for its "mystic poetry" and called "one of the most admirable paintings in the exhibition."

The show continued through Saturday, April 20, but two days before it ended, on Thursday evening in the lavishly beautiful Academy of Music in downtown Philadelphia, the Mendelssohn Club, which Wallace's father had founded in 1875 and which he had conducted ever since, presented the last performance of its 1906–1907 season. Most likely Wallace and Lucretia were among the audience because his father had written a new Sacred Cantata entitled *An Easter Idyll*, which the Club performed that evening. The senior Gilchrist was then sixty-one years old and still very much in his prime, the preeminent Philadelphia musician of the day. When the reviews came out praising his work and his conducting, it must have made that particular spring an especially proud one for the Gilchrist family.

Although Gilchrist made his living painting the well-to-do, one of his finest portraits is of a Cundy's Harbor neighbor, which he called *Uncle John* (see page 6). Early

*At Home, 1918*

*In Her Boudoir*

in the twentieth century a black man living on the Maine coast was a rarity. Down from Brunswick, on the dirt road to Cundy's Harbor, there was a shack a few hundred yards up from the Gilchrist place, and living there was an old black man everyone called Uncle John. His parents had been slaves, his wife was a full-blooded Indian, and he made his meager living doing everything from digging graves to digging for clams. For two dollars a day he would work at whatever odd jobs Gilchrist could offer. Bill described him as a gentleman with a large vocabulary who had met and impressed a number of well-educated people.

The result of this association was one of the most hauntingly beautiful portraits the artist ever did, capturing in the face of one man the pathos, strength, and dignity of the black race in America. It is unquestionably one of Gilchrist's greatest paintings. It is also yet another example of what the artist could do when not under the constant pressure to put bread on his family's table. Indeed, working as a portraitist meant that he was limited aesthetically, but works done on his own time offered what every artist needs—the time and scope to develop his talents without the constant awareness that someone's ego was hanging on every stroke of his brush.

*Girl in Pink* is not the only painting of Gilchrist's to leap from obscurity into the public eye. In 1932 the Milwaukee Art Institute was robbed of seven of its paintings, six on one occasion, and one week later Gilchrist's *Study of a Nude*.

In the short life of Wallace Gilchrist, a list of red-letter days would have to include Friday, February 26, 1915. On this winter day a ceremony held somewhere in Cumberland County in the State of Maine caused an old and beautifully located farmhouse on the Cundy's Harbor Road in the village of East Harpswell to be transferred from the hands of Mr. and Mrs. John Rawstron into the possession of W. Wallace Gilchrist, Jr., of Philadelphia for the sum of "one dollar and other valuable consideration." This additional valuable consideration allegedly came from the pocketbook of Mrs. Herbert Lloyd of Montclair, New Jersey (Mrs. Lloyd's maiden name was Anna Lord; she was a sister of Lucretia Gilchrist's mother, Ellen Lord deSchweinitz). Mrs. Lloyd thus became the family's most important benefactor, making possible the ownership of real estate for a man who had always paid rent.

Bill remembered that while cruising Quahog Bay in the family motor launch *Ermine*, probably during the summer of 1914, the Gilchrists had grown thirsty while exploring and spied four magnificent elm trees lined up in a row next to a pretty farmhouse a few hundred yards from the water. They landed, tied up, and walked up the grassy path to the house where, after satisfying their thirst, they discovered to their delight that the farmhouse was for sale.

Built in 1845 by Ezra Philbrick, a ship's carpenter who may have worked at Snow's shipyard on the nearby New Meadows River, the Federal cape was snug and long and built to be comfortable in all seasons for man and cows alike. The hayloft lay above the dirt-floored cow stable and was attached to, though not directly accessible from, the farmhouse. In Wallace's mind, it was immediately transformed into a studio. All it lacked was northern light and a staircase from outside, both of which were added in the course of the next eighteen months. The studio became precisely what Wallace had in mind in a letter he wrote from Holland to his father on New Year's Day, 1901, when he emphasized that his studio must be a "tempting environment."

Indeed, not only his studio but the entire coastal area where they would live could, at the very least, qualify as tempting. The meticulously detailed journalism of the weekly *Record* enables us to peek into the private lives of hundreds of area residents. For the editor and staff of this remarkable weekly, who assiduously collected information and paid by the inch for news of the personal lives of their readership, no detail was too minor for publication. One day in November of 1921, for example, we learn that a "Miss Gladys Olm and Miss Marrion Hill (of Bath) walked to Brunswick," certainly no mean feat in those days of poor dirt roads through largely empty countryside. Nor were the staff content with purely factual reportage, as the following, dated August 13, 1915, indicates: "A warning," shouts the headline: "If the woman who was seen taking flowers from different graves in Pine Grove Cemetery Sunday morning between the hours of 8 and 9 o'clock is seen to do the same thing again, her name will appear in the *Brunswick Record* on the first page in very large capital letters."

Knowing how dearly people love to see their names in print, every Thanksgiving the editors encouraged its readers to send in the names of their guests (a temptation to which the Gilchrists never succumbed). In 1921, for example, it required two issues of the *Record* to list all 294 people who submitted their guest lists. On January 26, 1917, it printed the names of the proud people who had cars on order at the Motor Mart, and when Nelly graduated from the ninth grade, we learn from the *Record* of June 17, 1921, that she prepared the onions for the graduation dinner.

For the Gilchrists, who spent most of their winters between 1915 and 1926 comfortably settled in various beautiful old homes in Brunswick or Topsham, the *Record* provides an entire historical and social context. From the pages of this weekly we can see, for instance, how wonderfully convenient it was to have rail service coming into Brunswick and connecting with Boston and all the major cities of the nation, as well as north to Lewiston/Auburn and Augusta and east to Rockland.

We find also that between the decline of rail passenger service and the maturity of roads for car and freight traffic was sandwiched a now-lost mode of transport known as the electric street railway, the so-called "electrics." A trolley ran on rails under an electrified wire all the way from Portland to Brunswick, where it branched, as did the railroad, to Lewiston and to Bath and Rockland. It carried freight as well as people, even loads of coal in the days prior to oil burners. The tracks were ripped up or abandoned when roads supplanted them, but old photos clearly show the rails and the electrified overhead wire paralleling the dirt and later the macadam roads.

During the eleven-odd years the artist and his family lived in Maine, he was fortunate to reside in a place as pleasant as Brunswick, where Bowdoin College, a group of dedicated and farsighted town fathers, and a location in one of the outstanding vacation spots of the world ensured a yearly migration in and out of the area, bringing a rich infusion of new faces and talents, not to mention money.

By today's standards Brunswick in 1915 was fairly primitive. Maine Street, for instance, despite being the widest in the state, was surfaced with dirt. By turns this became dust, mud, slush, ice, or some unpleasant and often treacherous combination as it was trod by pedestrians, who had no sidewalks, or by horses pulling wagons. Occasionally a newfangled horseless carriage drove the horses into a runaway frenzy. Add to this the electric trolley, horseback riders, and the tracks of the Maine Central, which cut straight across the street and held up traffic with interminable freight trains, and one begins to imagine the mess.

In 1910 the *Record* published a photo taken of all the cars in Brunswick, lined up proudly on Maine Street, no more than twenty-five of them in a single wide snapshot. By 1915 the paper was excitedly forecasting a fabulous future for cars, both here and in the entire world. In 1916 Brunswick was the second largest town in Maine, and a new "federal road" surfaced with gravel instead of dirt was nearly completed all the way to Portland. Even if automotive engineering were primitive enough to require a speed limit of twenty-five miles per hour, it was exciting and adventurous for the few who could then afford a car. Much that happened in those years was intensely exciting, as for example the first transcontinental phone call from Boston to San Francisco, written up in banner headlines in January 1915.

While President Wilson struggled to keep the nation out of the war raging in Europe, the Brunswick town fathers, several of whom were on the Bowdoin faculty, were pushing to attract "good, clean industry" to the town, to get Maine Street paved in concrete, to extend the mall southward by the Bowdoin campus, and to develop the large McKeen and Douglas estates just west of the campus into the prime residential areas they are today.

www.meyersphoto.com

*Studio Interior: The Artist and His Daughter Nelly*

*Summer Sunshine*

Between October and April in these northern latitudes the majority of human activity is forced indoors, but if we can trust the veracity of the *Brunswick Record*, no one could complain of boredom. Lucretia Gilchrist, as the wife of a prominent artist with wide and unpredictable fluctuations of income, had far less leisure time than did most women in her social set. Nevertheless, she somehow found the time and energy to make herself visible and helpful at scores of social functions, as did her two pretty daughters, both of whom were in their teens by 1919. She belonged, for example, to the Saturday Club, which sponsored all manner of dramatic, charitable, cultural, recreational, and social events. Membership in this club alone would have guaranteed a busy social life.

In those days the lack of modern appliances, the tradition keeping women busy at home, and the easy availability of inexpensive domestic help created a leisure class populated chiefly by women. Add to this a strong work ethic and a stimulating intellectual environment due to Bowdoin College, and the result is Brunswick society in 1915. It was this social milieu into which the Gilchrists plunged after moving up from Philadelphia, and the record shows that either Lucretia or Peggy or Nelly, and sometimes Wallace himself, represented the family at scores of functions. Whether acting as waitresses, helping to organize an exhibition of Gilchrist's works at the Bowdoin College art museum, entering a spring fashion show, participating in a dramatic production, or simply presiding over the refreshments table, one or more of the Gilchrist women took part.

How did this family of five manage, on an artist's uncertain income, to blend so well into the social fabric of Brunswick? First of all, Gilchrist in 1915 was a well-established painter with a national reputation in portraiture. Wealthy sitters paid well, and some prosperous people sat for Gilchrist, among them several members of the prominent Payson family, who have done so much over several generations to endow the Portland Museum of Art. There are no financial records of the artist's earnings, but although there were some times when Gilchrist made a handsome commission, and in one winter could hire maids at 75 Federal Street, Peggy always emphasized when talking about her family how careful her mother was about money. Her favorite expression was always, "Grandma had to scrimp and save." *

Then there is the "native son" factor. Although Gilchrist was born and educated and spent half his career in Philadelphia, Brunswick was only too eager to adopt him as their resident artist. The town was a lot smaller then, having only about 7,000 inhabitants compared to some 21,000 today. People were better informed about each other, largely due to the assiduously detailed reportage of the *Record*, and they found entertainment and recreation in each other's company. The only entertainment media were radio and the silent film, though the telephone and telegraph and an extensive transportation system were in some ways far better than today's. In this setting the Gilchrists soon became known as a family with three lively and attractive children of school age, and with a wife and mother deeply involved in the community.

This particular community, however, was not permeated by the mercenary spirit found in large cities such as New York or Boston. Owners of large old homes in downtown Brunswick near the college would rent their homes in the winter and travel abroad, and the Gilchrists were welcome tenants for a nominal rent. In this way Wallace could station his family in the less primitive surroundings of the area's cultural center near his most likely clientele. Every fall between 1915 and 1923, except for 1922, when they lived in Portland, the family moved to a different home in Brunswick or Topsham. In 1923 Wallace was finally able to install a furnace and heating system at Roadside and used his beloved Stutz Bearcat for the eight-mile trip to town. Necessity forced him to be as adept at heating systems and cars as he was with a paintbrush: he rebuilt the motor of his Bearcat and installed the furnace at Roadside with his own hands.

The Gilchrists were also helped by the cheapness of land and labor. Land was cheap simply because there was so much of it, and today the long, harsh winter repels all but the hardiest of souls and has kept the state uncrowded. Labor was cheap nationwide because of the enormous transatlantic migration of over forty million of Europe's dispossessed during Wallace's lifetime. In Brunswick, the labor supply was also swollen by Canada's poor French-speaking farmers, who, having used up the barren soils of southern Quebec, were easily lured to the mills along the Kennebec and the Androscoggin, where they inflated the labor supply not only with male and female mill workers but also with wives and children who were looking for ways to advance their status.

With labor thus relatively cheap it was possible to produce many low-priced necessities: early in 1915 a small house with five rooms on Pleasant Street was rented for $5 a month. Senter's store had a sale on all-wool skirts for 98¢ each, Benjamin Furbish offered airtight woodburning stoves, double-lined, for $1.90, marked down from $2.50. A worker at the Cabot Mill made about $40 a month, and his wife could buy hamburger for 18¢ a pound, a head of lettuce for a dime, and coffee for 22¢ a pound, all in the middle of January. If he and his wife and children were careful about saving and worked hard, and if his wife hired out as a cook or a maid for a Bowdoin professor or a local merchant, the family might save enough to buy a car. A Maxwell went for $695 ($750 with an electric starter).

A young teenager from nearby Durham might attend Brunswick High School for $8 a term. Finally, in January of 1915, the state legislature considered a bill to reduce the legal work week from sixty to fifty-four hours (six nine-hour days) and to forbid employment of females under age eighteen or males under sixteen. The so-called Protestant work ethic flourished in those days with a vengeance, but Catholics and Protestants alike labored grimly in bondage to it.

To all these advantages must be added the one factor that always tipped the scales in favor of the Gilchrists' survival—Lucretia, the artist's ever-inventive and resourceful wife. For years after Wallace died, her older daughter, Peggy, never tired of telling of the countless ways her mother scrimped and saved to keep the family going. Bill also always described her as a superb manager. If Wallace went out of town to do a commission, she was left to manage the household and the children and to deal with endless demands on her time and patience.

As a member of the old and venerable First Parish Church, probably the oldest institution in Brunswick and certainly the physically dominant one, its tower soaring upward at the summit of Maine Street, Lucretia helped out with all manner of church business. The women of the church were encouraged to join the Madisses Club, composed of madams and misses of the congregation. Sometimes they met just to talk and plan. They would sew for the Children's Home in Augusta or hold a Valentine Party

*Wildflowers on Ragged Island*

to raise money. For Valentine's Day of 1922, forty of them staged a fashion parade at the old Town Hall on Maine Street. Lucretia won first prize for her gown. Then there was the townwide Saturday Club, founded on January 12, 1895, by and for women. Although it sponsored a variety of events, it appears to have favored dramatic and musical productions. In March 1920 they produced *A Maid's Choice*, which Wallace's own father had written, and in November 1921 they staged *The Runaways*, which the *Record* called one of the best amateur productions in twenty-five years.

As the two Gilchrist sisters blossomed into adolescence, they represented the family by serving food and drink at countless events sponsored by local groups, including the Madisses, the Saturday Club, Community House, the Brunswick Club, the First Parish Church, and the Brunswick High School Athletic Association. In 1922, when Nelly was sixteen, she was thrilled to be asked to help the patronesses of Beta Theta Pi, one of the college fraternities, as they celebrated Ivy Day, one of two times during the academic year when the all-male student body was allowed to entertain female friends, many of them from out of town. In 1926, when Peggy was twenty-two and had just finished her junior year at Russell Sage College in Troy, New York, she was one of several Brunswick girls invited by midshipmen from Annapolis to a ball held at City Hall in Portland.

Dramatic productions, church suppers, fraternity socials, and dancing with midshipmen were by no means the only source of fun or social advancement. Judging by the prizes they won, both Lucretia and her daughter Nelly were no slouches at auction bridge. Then there was the Brunswick Club's annual tournament, where gamesters

*Dock on Bethel Point Road*

played pool, billiards, auction bridge, cribbage, and something called "63." On the memorable evening of February 1, 1922, Carroll York scored an upset victory in billiards by defeating Wallace 100–98. Because all seventy-five players were divided into two teams, the Snowflakes and the Hatchets, the result of the evening's carnage was being contested even as the *Record* went to press. The Snowflakes won 9–8, making Gilchrist's loss a sad one for the Hatchets.

The competitive fun also spilled out into the sparkling cold of a Maine winter just nine days later at the Winter Carnival held in nearby Bath, the climax of which was a race over the packed snow and ice of the two fastest horses in the state, followed by the annual ball at the Armory. That winter of 1922 was also memorable for a special Saturday evening at the end of January, when Peggy joined fifteen other girls and seventeen boys on two sleighs drawn by teams of four horses on a three-hour ride through the whitened winter landscape from Brunswick to Freeport. They left as the sun was setting, had dinner at a Freeport hotel, danced away the night, and even took in a movie before riding back through the dark frigid night to Brunswick.

On New Year's Eve 1919, the Gilchrists invited three family members to dinner. Wallace apparently had some skill in rhyming and for this occasion wrote eight limericks, one for each member of his immediate family, one for "Carl" (possibly a Gilchrist), one for "Grandma" (Susan Beaman Gilchrist), and one for a mysterious Aunt Mary (Carl's wife?):

There once was an Admiral Bill
Who lost all his teeth on a hill!
He slid from the top
To below without stop
On his jaw, which is quivering still.

Peggy, of course we all know
Is a bud, into bloom soon to blow.
She's approaching sixteen,
And is perfect as seen
From her head to her frost bitten toe.

There was a young girl named Nelly
Who was terribly fond of jelly,
She ate it so much
That it gave her a clutch
In the middle of her round little belly.

Uncle Carl is a man of great parts
Proficient in all of the Arts.
From the raising of Hens,
And pigs in their pens,
To the Ford and its intricate parts.

There once was a lovely Aunt Mary
Who never was ever contrary.
When asked out to dine,
She'd show up at nine!
With excuses quite likely to vary.

And Grandma, the sweet little dear—
Come so far, to be with us here!
Brings with her a smile
For each one of the miles
She has traveled, to start the New Year.

There once was a wonderful mother
Who was bound to make everyone love her.
She cooked all the dinner
And didn't grow thinner
For a part of the dinner was in her.

*Artist's Camping Tent*

Times like this give the lie to people who think the "good old days" never existed. Read the *Record*, where the sheer exuberance and humanity lie right between the lines for anyone with imagination to perceive. These Mainers had charm and warmth and strength, and they deeply cherished their little town. Wallace and Lucretia had chosen well, and even today, eighty years later, Brunswick is among the favorite places in the nation for retirees. The college and its proximity to Portland make the town a surprisingly sophisticated community by the Atlantic.

*After the Gilchrists began receiving some help from Albert Strauss and his wife and later from his daughter, Anna Lord Strauss (exactly when is unknown), they could afford more gracious living. Bill remembered that during the winter of 1917–1918, when they lived in the large house at 75 Federal Street (now occupied by the president of Bowdoin College), they employed two sisters, Edith and Gladis Curtis, who were then in their early twenties. In Bill's words, they "alternately lived in, working fast and efficiently from 5 A.M. until 8 P.M. with two hours off in the afternoon. All laundry was done by their mother in her home two miles away. The dining room table was set formally with Canton china and silver three times a day. To call service my mother would press a button by her toe that buzzed in the kitchen. At dinner the fireplace and candles were always burning. At least once a week there were one to four guests that might be Bowdoin College students, the age of my sisters (who were the attraction), or professors—sometimes President Sills and his wife and occasionally Governor Baxter's daughter Nelly—the age of my sister Nelly. And, of course, well-known artists who usually reciprocated with dinner invitations."

On Saturday, May 21, 1920, Western Union transmitted tragic news from Oakland, California, to the mother of Charles Allyn Gilchrist at 1618 Latimer Street, Philadelphia. Although the original telegram now looks fragile and yellowed with age, some eighty years later the words of Night Letter 2209 are easily legible. The text was composed by the woman who tried desperately to save the life of Charles Gilchrist:

Oakland California 21
Mrs W W Gilchrist
1618 Latimer St Philadelphia Penn
Charles Gilchrist drowned near Montara twenty miles south of San Francisco four o'clock yesterday afternoon exact cause accident unknown struggle short in heavy sea beating against precipictous [sic] rocks shore line being patrolled but body not yet recovered will wire any developments further information by mail we extend sincerest sympathy
Heck

Wallace's older daughter Peggy always spoke in a voice filled with awe and love whenever Uncle Charlie's name came up. Peggy was a lady essentially romantic in nature but disciplined enough to live responsibly. However, to question her about Uncle Charlie was always to invite a long discourse almost religious in tone. She took great romantic pleasure from the mere recitation of Charlie's life and achievements. One had the impression that had Peggy been born a man, she would gladly have emulated Uncle Charlie's life.

What exactly was it about this drowned man, the beloved genius and older brother of the artist, which during his forty-six years so enthralled and captivated those who knew him? And why, in a book about Wallace is it essential to know about Charlie, who spent so much of his life in pursuits and struggles which carried him so far afield from Germantown?

Consider what his chief mourners had to say, starting with Kathryn Heck, the woman who tried so valiantly to rescue him. She was his business partner, with a financial interest in and deep fascination for Charlie's last great dream, a project in which he strove with limited resources to create a motion picture of himself scaling the dramatic cliffs and chasms of the California coast. While in pursuit of this elusive goal, he became close friends with Kathryn and her husband. He boarded in their home in Berkeley and went out from there to attempt, with Kathryn's help, a task that today would surely require a whole crew of technicians, costly equipment, and possibly stunt men.

Given the technical brilliance of this remarkable man, who had a degree in civil engineering and could master just about any challenge he decided to confront, and given also his record of accomplishments, especially as a mountaineer with an international reputation, one can only wonder why his success in this final quest was so elusive. The answer, as so often was the case with all the Gilchrists, seems to have been twofold: lack of money and poor health.

Charlie complained in letters to his close friend Ross Burnham, who lived down the coast in Ramora in San Diego County, that his unfortunate purchase of cheap photographic equipment instead of the superior Bell and Howell product cost him far more in time, frustration, and repairs than he saved initially. When his health began to fail, for reasons never specified, he became more and more unhappy. His drive to complete his project became desperate. This was to be his great achievement, his crowning moment; he saw himself selling the finished film to Hollywood and becoming famous, perhaps even wealthy. Wealth and fame were ever the dream of the Gilchrist men, and they all came unbearably close.

Kathryn, having failed to rescue her friend from drowning, must have known heartbreaking agony, but the long letters she wrote to Charlie's mother and sister, carefully preserved by Charlie's nephew, Edmund B. Gilchrist, Jr., contain far more praise and love for Charlie than grief and self-pity for herself and her husband.

The first letter was to Charlie's mother, widow of the musician who had died three and a half years earlier. Susan Beaman Gilchrist lived alone above the office of her third son, Teddy, then thirty-five years old and married to Anita Sheppard. Kathryn's letter is a small jewel of tact and descriptive power as she tells the story of Charlie's drowning. To obtain the most objective story of the accident, however, one must read Mr. Heck's version, which he sent to the Alpine Club of America. It is far too long to include here in full, but the closing paragraph summarizes the romantic and glamorous side of this complex and gallant man:

Mr. Gilchrist was a member of the American Society of Civil Engineers, his unusual ability as a designer having been recognized both in the United States and on the Philippine Islands, where he spent several years in the service of the Government of the Philippine Islands, and a member of the Alpine Club of America, his hobby of mountain climbing having taken him to the summits of Mount Shasta of California, Hood of Oregon, Rainier of Washington, Ixtacihuatl and Popocatapetl of Mexico, the Matterhorn and other peaks of Switzerland, and to a point rarely reached on the slopes of Kanchanjunga, the second highest peak in the world in the Himalayas of Northern India.

Although Mr. and Mrs. Heck wrote separate versions of the drowning, all the information would have come from Kathryn Heck, who was the sole witness. Her husband merely helped present the story more fully. He also wrote in a more formal and restrained style. He begins with a careful description of the topography of the particular spot on the coast where the drowning occurred and builds from this a very lucid and thorough account.

Charles Gilchrist, as one might expect, was an experienced and powerful swimmer. When he told Kathryn Heck he wanted to revisit a spot close to the water to locate a "camera position for a picture which he had intended for some time to take," he evidently remembered having taken a refreshing "plunge into the sea at the same point on a previous trip," for he asked her to wait for him at the top of the promontory that afternoon late in May, overlooking the Pacific Ocean some 200 feet above the water. Then, having descended the almost sheer face of this cliff to a "comparatively level bench or shelf a short distance above the water," he may have decided to bathe in one of the shallow, tub-like cavities filled with warmed sea water thrown there by the waves, for Kathryn found his clothing there when she responded a few minutes later to his cry for help.

After descending the cliff as fast as she dared, she found to her horror that Charlie was close to drowning. She grabbed his clothing to make a lifeline, but the woolen puttees she knotted together parted under the strain when he clutched them. She frantically removed her own sweater and belt and fashioned a second lifeline. There was, however, absolutely nothing she could use as a purchase or anchor. She had to lean far out over the seething waves to dangle the lifeline. Charlie must have seen in that instant that should he somehow miraculously manage to grab the lifeline, there would be not one drowning but two. He disregarded the elusive lifeline and, too weakened by the frigid waters to waste energy talking, made no response to Kathryn's shout. By now he had been struggling naked in that hellish water for at least five minutes and probably longer, all the while being whipped about like driftwood by the fury of the waves that pounded through the long tunnel tapering inward at the base of the promontory.

As Kathryn stood helplessly, wondering whether Charlie had refused the lifeline because of his sense of chivalry, the water suddenly surged through the tunnel with a wave so massive that it carried the doomed swimmer backward, away from her. For a moment he disappeared entirely, then suddenly reappeared in a cove beyond the tunnel entrance. Kathryn heard him moan just once before glimpsing his body, lifeless now, floating in the open sea. She later reflected that he might have been killed at that moment by the tremendous force of the wave smashing him against the tunnel wall. The horror she had witnessed had taken no more than a minute. Charlie had disappeared and was never seen again.

To read the sympathy letters that the family received is to begin to understand that wherever Charlie went he carried with him a certain radiance. The Hecks, having been at the scene of the tragedy, were so badly shaken that they seriously considered moving away from Berkeley. So much of Charlie was there in their home—his equipment, memories of his charm and gentleness, and of the brave struggle he made to finish his grand project, and the constant knowledge that something or someone might have saved him from the icy fury of the Pacific.

Had Kathryn not plunged herself into the consuming task of editing Charlie's film for the movie market, they might well have sold out. As the spring of 1920 merged into summer, the letters she wrote the Gilchrists spoke glowingly of the beauty of Charlie's work. When the editing was done, she enthusiastically promoted the search for a buyer. Her one dominating concern was that his toils not be wasted, but despite all of her efforts no document has come to light showing what happened to the film.

Fortunately, the letters of five of the people who were closest to Charlie have survived. Ross Burnham and Hanford Henderson each wrote a pair of letters. Ross was probably related to the Mrs. Burnham who sent Wallace some money in 1901 so that he could extend his European trip, while Hanford Henderson is probably the "Dr. Henderson" who sailed in the *Statendam* with Wallace, Harry, and Joe in the fall of 1900.

C. Hanford Henderson* wrote two letters from his home in Keswick, Virginia. The first is a short but profoundly felt letter of sympathy to Anna. A week later, on May 29, he wrote a much longer letter, a very revealing one. Charlie, he says, "was the most talented of my two or three thousand boys," a statement implying that Dr. Henderson may have been headmaster of a school or even a professor at the University of Pennsylvania, which Charlie attended on scholarship after graduation from the Philadelphia Manual Training School. He was just twenty when he finished at Penn in 1893 with a Bachelor of Science degree, majoring in mining engineering.

In this letter Henderson sees the tragedy as a terrible waste of Charles's enormous but still unrealized potential, saying, "I did not like his going to the Philippines (as a civil engineer), and I was not at all satisfied with his life in California. I felt, as perhaps you did, that Charles was taking his life on too meagre terms, and that with his great ability and his large and varied talents, his personal charm and accomplishments, he deserved something much more brilliant and satisfying, in a word some destiny that corresponded with his great powers."

In sharp contrast to Dr. Henderson's high-minded dreams and expectations for Charlie, Ross Burnham writes a letter that marks him as one of Charlie's contemporaries. In an informal and down to earth letter to Anna, he uses Charlie's nickname, saying, "With Dads' going I have lost the very best friend I ever had. . ." and in his second letter, "Charlie's going has been a very great blow to me and I cannot even now realize it."

The two most moving letters, however, came from Charlie's two brothers. In a letter to Anna two weeks after the drowning, Ted refers to something unspecified she must have sent him to read: "That which you left me to read passes all imagination. I cannot tell you the feelings it gave, and will, for as long as I shall live. There is something grand about it, and, as it had to be, something very fitting as a way for Charlie to leave this earth, poor chap. Well, I can say no more. My deepest love to Moid."

And finally, on May 23, Wallace and Lucretia write messages combined into one letter. In the effort to console they go beyond their sorrow and convey news of their doings, as if to say life goes on and we are still here for you.

Dear Moid and Anna,
It all seems so impossible. I simply cannot grasp it at all—and suppose you must be suffering from the same feeling. And I feel for Moid in not having gotten out there to see Charlie as she wanted to. In one way it is not so hard to bear as it might have been, for he has been away so long that it eases the blow for us. But that doesn't make it any the less sad for him. He was too young to go so soon. At any rate it was sudden—and I guess that is our consolation—better than a dragged out illness. It is good to think that Ross, his old friend, was there.

I want to get out his photographs now and have them about, and think about his odd ways and funny stories. And I am going to get a kitten as a memorial. Greylegs has sprained his leg out of sympathy it seems. Well you had better get in your Ford and come down here pretty soon. It is getting warmer, and everything is in bud.

Billy is at the farm with L. and me—and the girls in B. still going to school. We may take them out after the 1st of June as Mrs. M. doesn't want them in the house any more. Nelly takes her lunches at the Smiths and Peggy at the Haskells. Very kind neighbors. The *Ermine* goes in the water soon and when you come we'll have some nice rides in her.
With lots of love, Wallace

Now Lucretia adds her message:

I am more sorry than I can say that this sudden blow has come for you to bear. We shall hope to hear more soon. Ross being so near, will do everything he can, I'm sure, to ease your mind, but it must be dreadfully hard to be so far away. Billy, Nelly & I have just rowed down to Diamond Point, & walked up to see the Choates—Now they have come up in their car & taken W. & Billy off trout fishing. Last week I went down to meet Margt., who came in on the 15th. I stayed with her at Aunt Anna's [Mrs. Herbert Lloyd] until Tues. reaching home again Wed. Am running two houses now. Margt. looks and is just exactly the same—perhaps a little thinner—She won't be here until later. Her friend [?] Mitchell is a fine girl.
Lovingly, Lucretia

Charles Gilchrist, in addition to being an extraordinary man who left his mark wherever he went, was one of the two men who most strongly influenced Wallace. Their father was unquestionably the most powerful force acting on both of them, but the older brother's genius and sheer physical daring set an impossibly high standard which, as a boy, Wallace strove to match. It is entirely possible that this early rivalry, however good-natured it may have been, put too much strain on Wallace's heart at a time when little was known about congenital heart defects.

In any case, while Charlie saw life as a series of mountain peaks waiting to be conquered, Wallace realized as he reached manhood that no matter how grandly he aspired, his heart could and often did limit his activities. The strain of marriage, children, friends, an active social life to support his professional network, frequent travel, a harsh climate, unceasing financial anxiety, and, as we shall see, air pollution as virulent as any in the world, all combined with a career demanding the utmost from him and exacted a very heavy toll on his heart.

Sometimes it was simple frustration that upset him the most. Bill told about the time his father exerted himself helping a friend launch a boat, only to return to Roadside so exhausted that it took three days to recover his strength. Although Bill remembers one occasion when his father actually wept with misery in front of the family, he very seldom complained. He possessed marvelous self control, though he would usually lose it when Nelly played the radio too loud.

People who knew him well said he was blessed with a personality at once sparkling with life and wit but under the control of a quiet resignation and a gentle serenity. He never knew what it was like to have an enemy. He tried to understand people, so that even the most cantankerous individual would never provoke him. This was probably good for his health, good for his reputation, and good for his conscience and peace of mind.

*There was a C. Hanford Henderson who served as headmaster of the Pratt Institute in Brooklyn, New York, in 1887, the year the school was founded. Like Charlie, he was a mining engineer and by 1920 could have been retired and living in Keswick, Virginia.

I n July 1924, a marvelous opportunity was offered to Wallace by the prestigious Carnegie Institute in Pittsburgh, Pennsylvania. It flattered his ego, but, more importantly, promised a decent and regular income. Wallace accepted the offer and agreed to serve as associate professor of painting and illustration. Lucretia must have been thrilled at the prospect of a comfortable and secure life, and one can imagine a very busy two months in the old farmhouse as the Gilchrists prepared to make a major move.

Wallace in 1924 was a well-known and well-traveled man, having made two voyages to Europe in his twenties and innumerable trips up and down the eastern seaboard, especially between Philadelphia and Maine. However, neither he nor Lucretia had lived in Pittsburgh, and what happened in that muscular metropolis on the western side of the Appalachians was almost predictable: a hard working and accomplished artist with a national reputation attempted a job that his afflicted heart could not support.

He and Lucretia took with them young Bill, then on the threshold of puberty, and they spent several weeks in an expensive hotel while Wallace began his teaching duties and Lucretia searched for a place to live. Bill remembered his mother being quite concerned to see young couples actually walking arm-in-arm in public. He also remembered that for him, the move from a rather rural community in Maine to the heart of Pittsburgh was a vastly stimulating experience. The young girls he saw there were a constant distraction, and their responses to his charm and good looks were enough to give his mother cause for concern.

After coming within a whisker of renting a choice apartment near the University, the Gilchrists finally found a pleasant place to live at 912 Ivy Street and settled in for the academic year.

The first month must have gone fairly well, but the weather soon turned colder, and the coal dust-laden air for which Pittsburgh was then so infamous began to bear down on him. Under the stress of a heavy teaching load and time-consuming but necessary social obligations, he became increasingly exhausted. By the end of October, he must certainly have begun to question whether he could complete the academic year without collapsing from the strain. In November it became painfully clear that he would have to resign and return to Maine.

The grim decision was made, and Lucretia went ahead alone by train to prepare the old farmhouse for Wallace's return. Young Bill stayed on in Pittsburgh for a few more days until his father was rested enough to attempt the journey home, then said good-bye to a place where beautiful girls had stirred his fantasies, a city where his father had been a much-liked teacher who was simply too sick to continue.

The doctors of that day would have bundled Wallace off to a warm climate or a mineral spa, such as he had once tried with remarkable success years before in Germany, but he came up sharply against his perennial lack of money. So the artist, who had gone off to a new adventure in the warmth of September, full of sparkling hope and optimism, was reduced to trundling by train and old Model T back up the cold leafless spine of the Northeast to his homestead in Maine.

The Gilchrists resigned themselves to staying on through the winter at the farmhouse, knowing that without a steady income and with the artist still too weak to travel, they could not afford to rent in Brunswick, as they had done every year from 1915 to 1922. Physically isolated from Brunswick's busy social life, the Gilchrists simply dug in and made the best of it.

Wallace found himself far out on a Maine peninsula, where he faced the bitter realization that his spirit had, once again, pushed his flesh too hard. The man who as a youngster had climbed flagpoles, whose older brother had scaled the Matterhorn, returned from Pittsburgh to the clean, cold air of the Atlantic. He was barely able to cross the living room at Roadside without suffering palpitations. There he settled in for the long Maine winter with no running water, no electricity, and at first only the faintest hope for recovery of enough vigor to continue his work as an artist.

What he did have, however, was love. Lucretia and Bill endlessly nursed and waited upon him. Friends and neighbors came by to help and encourage. His daughters, who were now eighteen and twenty, were away from home. Nelly was studying sculpture in Philadelphia, and Peggy was a sophomore at Russell Sage College. Luckily for Wallace and Lucretia, young Bill was still at home, and he soon became the indispensable young man of the house. He vividly recalled how he labored as a fourteen-year-old to work up seven cords of firewood and to carry water from the well a hundred yards uphill through the snow to the house, where it was heated on a wood stove and used to give his father the Nolheim bath in a tub in the laundry room.

Although the family was only seven miles from Brunswick, that winter at Roadside was isolated and primitive. Natives of the state are fond of saying that Maine has just two seasons, winter and July, and Bill always swore the temperature in their outhouse seldom rose above 20 below in January. In such weather the Model T would start only if the rear wheels were first jacked up before the engine was hand-cranked. The furnace, which Wallace had installed the year before on the earthen floor of the cellar, needed regular stoking and feeding, and the kerosene stoves they carried from room to room were dangerous, smelly, and smoky. Brunswick was at least half an hour away over winding dirt roads and across the narrow water called the Gurnet, which separates Great Island from the mainland.

As winter approached, Wallace slowly responded to the treatment prescribed by his doctor and to the ministrations of his wife and son. He was kept indoors by illness and weather, but this constriction of his routine benefited his work by forcing him to paint family and interior scenes. Today his reputation is built more on paintings of his family and on what art historians call New England interiors than on portraiture. In fact, it was during this period that he painted, in his own dining room at Roadside, the work he called *After Breakfast*, which was called a masterpiece when it was exhibited the following summer.

The irony of his last two years is that the illness that weakened him and eventually took his life also gave him the perfect excuse to paint for his own enjoyment and reputation rather than simply to put bread on his table. His ill health caused his family considerable hardship, but Wallace was first, last, and always an artist. He did his work, and there were times when everything and everyone else were secondary. Had he compromised too much, we would not have the wonderful work he left behind. Nor would his family and descendants and all of the people who sat for him have the deep satisfaction his work has given, and into which he put all he had.

## The Stutz Bearcat

**B**eing a painter may not always bring in regular or even sufficient income, but it does offer a certain marvelous freedom of action. No surly supervisor, no time clock to punch, and nothing but his own decision on how and where to spend his time—these are the perks of an artist's life, and as Wallace began the forty-sixth summer of his life, he enjoyed them to the fullest.

Having rebuilt his strength over the long winter at Roadside, in the summer of 1925 he bought a second-hand Stutz Bearcat touring car. Tired of driving the standard Model T, he apparently decided to take the risk of buying a used car, and after he had rebuilt the engine the Bearcat became one of his prized possessions. Just as the *Ermine* had become his special mode of transport by water, the Bearcat moved Wallace from point to point on land.

In July of that summer Peggy was twenty-one, Nelly almost nineteen, and Bill just shy of fifteen. All three children happened to be living at Roadside that month, so Wallace decided to invite them on a day trip to the White Mountains of New Hampshire. After surviving ten Maine winters, he had learned the lesson all native Mainers absorb at a tender age: never waste a Maine summer. He must have realized that with two daughters soon to become self-sufficient and already living away at school, the chance to take a trip with all three would not soon repeat itself.

He had just returned from a short visit to paint landscapes, so he had a particular New Hampshire resort in mind as their destination. Lucretia probably had things to do at home, and she habitually put Wallace's health and happiness ahead of her own. Besides, the back seat of the Bearcat was uncomfortable for three people. The day they picked was Wednesday, July 15. It dawned auspiciously warm and sunny, Maine weather at its best, ideal for touring with the top down.

Wallace packed them all into the car, and after Lucretia had kissed them all good-bye, making sure they hadn't forgotten their picnic lunches, off they roared in the Stutz to see the mountains. One thing a casual observer might have noticed as they headed into Brunswick to pick up the Portland Road that morning was the position of the driver: Wallace sat on the right-hand side. Otherwise they were just four of the thousands of people using the automobile to travel somewhere beautiful and refreshing during the all-too-brief summer in northern New England.

The next day was Thursday, the day the *Brunswick Record* came off the presses each week, so it must have taken some fast reportorial action and a quick writing job to put the following headline on the front page:

Brunswick Artist in Auto Collision Wednesday Evening
W. W. Gilchrist in Head-on Smash on Portland Road
Cars Demolished
Two autos met in head-on collision some time after nine o'clock Wednesday evening near Stone's Pond on the Portland Road. W. W. Gilchrist, well known artist, who has a summer home at East Harpswell, was traveling toward Brunswick in his Stutz touring car, being accompanied by his daughter Nelly. When at the point mentioned, a narrow strip of macadam, he met Emery Kinney of Fort Fairfield, driving in his Peerless touring car to Providence. The narrow road and blinding lights brought the cars together. Both were demolished. Miss Gilchrist was the only injured party and she was but badly shaken up.

In its haste to meet the press deadline, the *Record* got two facts wrong. Nelly was not injured, and she was not alone with her father. Although all four Gilchrists were shaken by the crash, only Peggy was hurt. Bill was sitting in the front to the left of his father, and Peggy sat directly behind her brother, thus placing Nelly behind her father who, as noted earlier, drove on the right-hand side, making it difficult to judge the path of oncoming cars.

In the darkness on that narrow road, Mr. Kinney also badly misjudged or could not see the path of the Stutz moving toward him, headlights blazing. He veered into Wallace's lane, forcing the artist far to the right and onto the ties of the electric railway line that ran between the road and the nearby body of water, since filled in, known as Stone's Pond.

Had the artist been fractionally less alert or a second slower in responding, the accident might easily have been fatal. As it was, the left front ends of the cars took the full impact and must have swerved somewhat, cushioning the impact. The left rear door of the Stutz popped open and Peggy, thrown out onto the pavement, was fortunate not to suffer more than a mild concussion requiring only a few days of bedrest. Ever afterward she would entertain people with the story of her narrow escape from death. When this writer was a teenager she used the story to good effect, once saying that the automobile was a "death dealing weapon."

Wallace and Emery, once the dust had settled and the shock had worn off, piled out of their cars and nearly had a fist fight. Wallace was furious and at the same time sick at heart. His beloved Bearcat was a total wreck, horribly mangled, beyond repair.

Before long a patrolman arrived and took the party of unhappy excursionists to Brunswick, where Lucretia was notified and arranged for a friend to fetch her family back to Roadside. As a result of the accident, Mr. Kinney's trip to Providence was cut short, the *Record* wrote one of its few inaccurate stories, Wallace was rendered utterly miserable, and the Gilchrist children survived to tell the story of the crash of the Bearcat for years afterward.

# BRUNSWICK, 1926

In the fall of 1925 the family tried a house in Topsham instead of Brunswick. It was called the Duncan House and is the setting for at least two of Wallace's New England interiors. Situated on a hill at 14 Green Street, the house faces Brunswick across the Androscoggin River. Behind it sits a large barn where Bill, then a strapping lad of fifteen, busied himself after school that winter building some fifty wooden lobster traps. He had big plans for the spring of 1926.

In May of 1926, Gilchrist took sick. He had turned forty-seven that March, and as he grew older he took longer to recover from illness. The family moved from Green Street back to Roadside, as was their custom every spring, but some time that summer they decided to return to Brunswick, where Wallace would be closer to his doctor and to the newly opened hospital on Union Street. The house they rented, and where he died, was on Oakland Street, just a few blocks west of Bowdoin College.

Few people outside his own family knew how sick the artist was. Many of his closest friends were in Philadelphia that summer and fall for the 150th anniversary celebration of the Declaration of Independence, also referred to as the Sesquicentennial. Among the spectacles that drew attention was a building for the exhibition of American painting, a must-see for painters that year.

A few of the letters Wallace received from friends in Philadelphia that fall describe the exhibition he was missing. This one, from this friend Carroll Tyson,* written on October 1, was one of the last he received:

Dear Wallace,

I hear that you have been very poorly and wish to tell you how awfully sorry I am to hear of it and as they say in Maine "and hopes this finds you improvin'." If you have had a fever your ears must have been the warmest part of you yesterday, for Bo and I & Alex Bower, Harding, Oberteuffer & Redfield were all standing in front of that portrait you did of the old man (not so old either, but white hair) and we all liked it tremendously—a damned fine portrait—congratulations!

If you were here today, we might go to the Casino & see the All Revue Beauty Show and have a good laugh. I haven't been there since you & I went there together and saw our mutual friend the drummer.

The Sesqui Show is certainly very good. It is like a glorified Academy show with splendid light and well hung. Redfield hung it so of course his own pictures are beautifully shown !! I have five landscapes there. In February I am at last to have a show at Durand of landscapes and in April a show at Wildensteins, NY of pastel nudes—all nudes. I have been doing a great number, destroying the ones that are not so good and keeping the ones that are better. How's that for a diplomatic way of putting it? My nephew Jim Bond and I expect to go hunting from Lee, Maine twelve miles down the Passadumkeag Stream by canoe. I am thrilled at the prospect. We are talking about you at the Sesqui and hoping for a speedy recovery. Bower said he was going to write you, so of course I couldn't let Alex get ahead of me, so I am writing to be first or at least I don't think he wrote last night. He gave us a drink of damned good whiskey which we needed as we were

*Artist's Daughters Peggy and Nelly*

exhausted going around looking at the exhibition. Today I expect to see my old friend Ethel Barrymore in "[?] Look," a curious name for a play. Well, Wally, good luck to you and get well soon. I am only too sorry that you have all this trouble. With [?] wishes to Lucretia and yourself.

From your "old" but true friend Carroll

On the same day, Alexander Bower wrote to tell Wallace that he had won a silver medal for his *Portrait of Stephen Matthews*.

In the last week of his life, near the end of October, Wallace received a letter from Stanley Kaufman from Newark, New Jersey. Evidently Kaufman, a novelist and friend, wished to dedicate a novel to Wallace, but the novel was a bit on the salacious side.

A tactful and considerate man, Wallace decided he should write and gently decline the honor. It is a sign of how sick he was that he dictated the letter to Lucretia. It was sent to Kaufman who, when he learned of Wallace's death, sent the letter to Teddy asking that it be returned. Fortunately, Teddy kept the letter.

The first three paragraphs inform Kaufman that Wallace declines the honor, because, as Wallace puts it, "there may be some people who will hesitate to leave the book on the drawing room table when children are in the room." In the fourth paragraph Wallace refers to some stag parties he and Kaufman attended.

But—Stanley—did you ever happen to think that we were in reality both of us very good boys—there was nothing ever very salacious in anything we did. Our suppers were always stag and the evenings as well—We never had the parties others had. But we had lots of fun. The love in all of your books is of the perfectly pure type. And I deny that my nudes are not the same. They are painted for all the Art—all the Beauty—I could get into them—there is the key note to all art—that is the guide. Always say: "Is it beautiful?" Now how is it possible to be beautiful and to be smutty, dirty, and salacious all at once. Leave the bathroom stuff to Bernard McFadden and his thousand henchmen. He takes care of both the pictorial and literary side for us. It is all stale.

On November 4, 1926, Peggy, who was in her last year at Russell Sage, said she suddenly knew from a distance of several hundred miles the very moment her father died. Call it telepathy, but this is the story she always told about one of the worst moments of her life.

The next day the *New York Times* ran a four-sentence obituary squeezed between a long description of Harry Houdini's memorial service and an equally extensive obituary of Annie Oakley. On the same day, Cousin Lewis wrote to Lucretia from Wellesley, Massachusetts:

My Dear Lucretia,
I was deeply grieved to read in tonight's paper of Wallace's going, and, while I knew he had been a very sick man, one never is prepared for these losses, and it came as a shock. You know, I am sure, that you have my deepest sympathy in your bereavement, and that I share most sincerely in your sorrow. Dear old Wallace was certainly one of the most lovable fellows I ever knew—the sort of cousin one could be fond of without thinking of relationship. While I esteemed and valued him most as a man, artist, and friend, I take pride in remembering that he was my cousin; and he reminded me strongly of my mother—the Gilchrist type is very persistent—that ties of blood were very real. How much I wish I might have seen him that day last summer—I little thought that I should never have another chance.

The last letter comes, fittingly, from a man whom Gilchrist painted, who was his friend and neighbor in Brunswick one winter when the family lived on Federal Street. His portrait now hangs in the downstairs hallway of the house on Federal Street where President Sills lived and where Gilchrist may well have painted the portrait.

Bowdoin College
Brunswick, Maine
November 21, 1926

Office of the President

My dear Mrs. Gilchrist,
Ever since your husband's death I have intended to write to you—not that letters are of avail but for my own sake that you may know how genuinely he will be missed. Mr. Gilchrist I have always liked ever since I first met him. We seemed to hit it off and I recall now with great satisfaction many a talk we had. When he was doing the wall portrait, I used genuinely to enjoy sitting for him—he always had so many ideas and was so intelligent not only about art but about

*Dock at Roadside*

things in general. Had he lived longer and been in good health I am confident he would have left a great name. As it is, his work seems to me to be very much above average and in some of his portraits I think he reached a very high standard indeed. It was such a real joy to have had him in our community.

The day of the funeral I prized the opportunity of being one of the bearers and I thank you for thinking of me. I was sorry that these days were so crowded with college business—I was in New York when your husband died—that I had to delay writing. You will, I know, accept my deep if belated sympathy and extend it to your daughters and your son. I still have in my desk and shall always treasure a letter Mr. Gilchrist wrote me last summer. Mrs. Sills desires to be included in this very inadequate message.
Believe me, very faithfully yours,
Kenneth M. Sills

Wallace died about 6:30 on Thursday evening, November 4, 1926. At noon on Saturday a funeral service was held at the house on Oakland Street, with both Reverend Thompson E. Ashby and Reverend Chauncey W. Goodrich officiating. His body was taken to Philadelphia, probably over the same rails he had traveled on his way to and from Pittsburgh. From the city he was taken to St. Thomas Church in Whitemarsh, which in that year was far out in the country north of the city. Here, in a lovely shaded spot on a small hill near the road, he was laid to rest in the family plot.

His work finally done, he rested.

*When Wallace's younger brother, Teddy, went into a deep depression in the early 1950s, Carroll Tyson, who was independently wealthy, arranged for him to live on Mt. Desert Island, providing a housekeeper and whatever else he needed. (The final years of Teddy's life bore an eerie resemblance to the last years of his father, the musician, spent in a sanitarium in Easton, Pennsylvania.)

# LIST OF EXHIBITIONS

Note: I have copied the titles as they were printed in exhibition catalogues of the time, so, as the catalogues are not consistent, one work may have several different titles in this list. PAFA is Pennsylvania Academy of the Fine Arts, and NAD is National Academy of Design. ACP is Art Club of Philadelphia, PSDW is Philadelphia School of Design for Women, and BCMA is Bowdoin College Museum of Art (called the Walker Art Museum in Gilchrist's lifetime). PSA is Portland (Maine) Society of Art, precursor to the Portland Museum of Art.

| DATE | LOCATION | CAT. # | TITLE |
|---|---|---|---|
| 1/20/–3/01/02 | PAFA | 449 | Portrait, Phillip H. Goepp |
| 1/23/–3/04/05 | PAFA | 218 | Portrait, Helen J. Sellars |
| | | 473 | Portrait, WWG, Musical Director |
| | | 737 | Grandfather's Prints |
| 1/22/–3/03/06 | PAFA | 518 | Still Life |
| | | 633 | Model's Rest |
| | | 654 | Portrait, Mr. B. DeSchweinitz |
| 1906 | Cincinnati | 72 | Model's Rest |
| 1906 | Chicago | | Model's Rest |
| 1/21/–2/24/07 | PAFA | 25 | Portrait, Miss Louise DeSchweinitz |
| | | 106 | Portrait, Mrs. Parrish |
| | | 461 | Portrait, Mr. E. G. McCollin |
| 3/16/–4/20/07 | NAD | 59 | Portrait, Mrs. Parrish |
| | | 90 | Portrait, Mr. E. G. McCollin |
| | | 117 | In the Studio |
| | | 250 | The Mirror |

| DATE | LOCATION | CAT. # | TITLE |
|---|---|---|---|
| 4/12/–4/20/07 | PSDW | | Spanish Dancing Girl |
| | | | Still Life |
| | | | Moonrise– Mount Desert |
| | | | Portrait of an English Bay |
| | | | At Play on the Sand Dunes |
| | | | A Portrait Study |
| | | | The Golden Screen |
| | | | Still Life |
| | | | The Wedding Gown |
| | | | Portrait of Miss Marion Wartman |
| | | | Portrait of Miss Louise DeSchweinitz |
| | | | Portrait of Dr. W.W.G. |
| | | | Westminster Abbey by Night |
| | | | Study |
| | | | The Yellow Chrysanthemum |
| | | | Still Life |
| | | | Portrait of Mr. Isaac Pennypacker |
| | | | Portrait of Mrs. Isaac Pennypacker |
| | | | Portrait of Mr. John McKeon |
| | | | The State House, Haarlem |
| | | | Hill Country– Susquehanna County |
| | | | The Little Pink Boarding House |
| | | | Still Life |
| | | | Prints |

| Date | Location | Cat. # | Title |
|---|---|---|---|
| | | | Portrait of Miss Priscilla Poor |
| | | | Portrait of Mr. Charles E. Drake |
| | | | Study of a Child |
| | | | Child's Head |
| | | | Portrait Study |
| | | | Portrait of W.W.G. |
| | | | Portrait of Mrs. Lord (unfinished) |
| | | | A Shimmer of Light |
| | | | Copy from F. Hals |
| | | | Copy from F. Hals |
| | | | Copy from Velásquez |
| 1907 | Cincinnati | 234 | The Mirror |
| | | 235 | Still Life |
| | | 236 | Our Fair Critic |
| | | 237 | Portrait, Alan D. Cochran |
| 1/20/–2/29/08 | PAFA | 16 | Portrait, Carl Pohlig |
| | | 156 | In the Little Gold Room |
| | | 301 | Portrait, Miss Mary Edgar |
| | | 375 | The Morning Mail |
| | | 729 | Portrait, Rev. Frank Sewall |
| 3/14/–4/18/08 | NAD | 209 | Daughter and Doll |
| | | 341 | In the Little Gold Room |
| 12/12/–1/09/09 | NAD | 17 | The Cottage Doorway |
| | | 312 | Portrait, Dr. Gilchrist |
| 1908 | Cincinnati | 108 | Le Boudoir Rose |
| 1908 | Chicago | 102 | Loving Stitches (watercolor) |
| 1908 | Chicago | 104 | Flirtation |
| | | 105 | The Farm Horse |
| | | 106 | The Mirror |

| Date | Location | Cat. # | Title |
|---|---|---|---|
| 1/31/–3/14/09 | PAFA | 10 | Creton Rose |
| | | 503 | A Study in Lavender |
| | | 529 | Model's Rest |
| | | 729 | Portrait |
| 11/01/–11/13/09 | McClees Galleries, Philadelphia | | The Kindergarten |
| | | | A Study in Blue |
| | | | The Letter |
| | | | By the Sea |
| | | | Le Boudoir Rose |
| | | | A Study in Violet |
| | | | Blue and Yellow |
| | | | Creton Rose |
| | | | The Old Gold Screen |
| | | | An Interior |
| | | | The Brook |
| | | | The Houses of Parliament, London |
| | | | Girl in White |
| | | | Nelly and Doll |
| | | | The Black Veil |
| | | | A Study in Lavender |
| | | | The Mirror in the Box |
| | | | Trimming Hats |
| | | | The Velvet Gown |
| | | | The White Skirt |
| | | | Tanagra |
| | | | Copy from Rubens |
| | | | Copy from Franz Hals |
| | | | Miss Anna Beaman |
| | | | Mrs. Parrish |
| | | | Katherine Strauss |
| | | | Dr. W. W. Gilchrist |
| | | | Dr. Edward Brooks |
| | | | Mr. Carl Pohlig |
| | | | Mr. John McKeon |
| | | | Margaret |
| 12/02/09–1/09/10 | NAD | 17 | Trimming Hats |
| | | 18 | Creton Rose |
| | | 104 | An Interior |
| | | 150 | The Kindergarten |

| Date | Location | Cat. # | Title |
|---|---|---|---|
| 1909 | Cincinnati | 108 | *Creton Rose* |
| | | 109 | *A Study in Blue* |
| | | 110 | *Girl in Brown* |
| | | 111 | *By the Light of the Lamp* |
| | | 112 | *The Cottage Doorway* |
| 12/20/09–1/16/10 | ACP | | *Velvet Gown* |
| | | | *Study in Violet* |
| | | | *Le Boudoir Rose* |
| 1/23/–3/20/10 | PAFA | 241 | *Portrait, Dr. E. Brooks* |
| | | 554 | *Through the Open Door* |
| 12/19/10–1/08/11 | ACP | | *Lady Lynx* |
| 3/12/–4/17/10 | NAD | 133 | *Study in Violet* |
| | | 210 | *The Fur Cape* |
| | | 392 | *Le Boudoir Rose* |
| 1910 | Chicago | 96 | *Le Boudoir Rose* |
| 1910 | Chicago | 91 | *At the Milliner's (pastel)* |
| 1910 | Cincinnati | 52 | *Mending* |
| 2/05/–3/26/11 | PAFA | 229 | *The Girl and the News* |
| | | 522 | *Portrait of Miss M* |
| 4/02/–4/13/11 | ACP | | *In the Music Room* |
| | | | *Daydreams (The Locket)* |
| 12/09/–1/07/12 | NAD | 211 | *Portrait of Miss M* |
| | | 279 | *A Study in Violet* |
| 1911 | Chicago | 140 | *In the Music Room* |
| | | 141 | *Girl Reading* |
| 1911 | Cincinnati | 45 | *Daydreams* |
| | | 46 | *In the Music Room* |

| Date | Location | Cat. # | Title |
|---|---|---|---|
| 2/04/–3/24/12 | PAFA | 109 | *Brown and Gold* |
| | | 165 | *Mrs. John K. Borland, Jr. in Dancing Costume* |
| 4/15/–5/12/12 | ACP | | *Cerise* |
| | | | *Brown Turban* |
| | | | *Beaching the Dory* |
| 9/15/12– | St. Louis | 46 | *The Old Japanese Screen* |
| 1912 | Chicago | 98 | *Blue and Gold* |
| | | 99 | *A Study in Velvet* |
| | | 64 | *Brown and Gold* |
| | | 65 | *Seated Figure and Screen* |
| | | 66 | *Figure Study against Screen* |
| | | 67 | *Portrait, Dr. W.W.G.* |
| | | 68 | *Peggy* |
| | | 69 | *Nelly* |
| 2/09/–3/30/13 | PAFA | 143 | *Portrait, Miss Ettel Barksdale* |
| 3/15/–4/20/13 | NAD | 62 | *The Old Gold Screen* |
| 12/20/13–1/18/14 | NAD | 255 | *Shadows* |
| 1913 | Chicago | 139 | *The Old Gold Screen* |
| 1913 | Cincinnati | 79 | *The Old Gold Screen* |
| | | 80 | *The Seamstress* |
| 2/08/–3/29/14 | PAFA | 216 | *The Studio Window* |
| 3/21/–4/26/14 | NAD | 39 | *Study in Green and Gold* |
| 11/03/–12/06/14 | Chicago | 124 | *Sunrise* |
| | | 125 | *Slumber* |
| 11/08/–12/13/14 | PAFA | | *6 watercolors* |
| 12/19/14–1/17/15 | NAD | 310 | *The Mirror* |

| DATE | LOCATION | CAT. # | TITLE |
|---|---|---|---|
| 1914 | Cincinnati | 76 | *The Mirror* |
| 1914 | American Watercolor Society of New York | | *The Incoming Tide* |
| 3/20/–4/25/15 | NAD | 408 | *A Study in Brown and Gold* |
| | | 426 | *A Colonial Hallway* |
| 1915 | Chicago | 137 | *The Mirror* |
| 1915 | Cincinnati | 32 | *The First and Third Generations* |
| 2/16/–3/26/16 | PAFA | 291 | *By the Window* |
| | | 298 | *The Pink Settee* |
| | | 329 | *Head* |
| 3/18/–4/23/16 | NAD | 320 | *Decorative Panel* |
| 9/13/16– | St. Louis | 62 | *The Mirror* |
| 11/02/–12/07/16 | Chicago | 115 | *Mother and Child* |
| | | 116 | *Little Nell* |
| | | 117 | *Decorative Panel* |
| 12/04/16 | BCMA | | *John Calvin Stevens Gilchrist Family at Breakfast* |
| 2/14/–3/25/17 | PAFA | 297 | *Mother and Baby* |
| | | 393 | *Mother and Child* |
| 3/17/–4/22/17 | NAD | 17 | *Mother and Child* |
| | | 252 | *The Model's Rest* * |
| 7/13/–9/16/17 | PSA | | *Mother and Baby* |
| 9/23/–10/28/17 | St. Louis | 60 | *The Gold Screen* |

| DATE | LOCATION | CAT. # | TITLE |
|---|---|---|---|
| 9/26/–10/22/17 | PSA | | *Knitting for the Soldiers* |
| | | | *A Quiet Hour* |
| | | | *A Visit to the Studio* |
| | | | *Sisters* |
| | | | *A Sunny Corner* |
| | | | *Morning Gossip* |
| | | | *Reverie* |
| | | | *The Grey Veil* |
| | | | *Charles H. Payson* |
| | | | *The Chimney Corner* |
| | | | *Bess* |
| | | | *Slumber* |
| | | | *At Anchor* |
| | | | *John Calvin Stevens* |
| | | | *Old Black Joe* |
| | | | *W. W. Gilchrist, Sr.* |
| 11/08/17–1/02/18 | Chicago | 77 | *A Visit to the Studio* |
| | | 78 | *Early Morning Gossip* |
| 3/13/–4/21/18 | NAD | 81 | *A Sunny Corner* |
| 12/11/18–1/12/19 | NAD | 64 | *In the Studio* |
| | | 147 | *The South Window* |
| 1918 | War Relief Fund | | *Mending the Flag* |
| 1919 | Chicago | 83 | *The Gold Screen* |
| 4/06/–5/19/20 | NAD | 229 | *The Fair Bookworm* |
| 6/11/20 | BCMA | | *Portrait, Professor Chapman* |
| 9/15/–10/31/20 | St. Louis | 83 | *The Little Seamstress* |
| 10/20/–11/21/20 | PSA | | OILS: |
| | | | *Sills, President of Bowdoin* |
| | | | *Manton Copeland, Jr.* |
| | | | *Arthur F. Brown* |
| | | | *Nellie Baxter* |
| | | | *George F. Noyes* |
| | | | *Sketch of My Boy* |
| | | | *Professor Henry L. Chapman* |
| | | | *N. Brook Smith* |
| | | | *Edwin T. Gignoux* |

| DATE | LOCATION | CAT. # | TITLE |
|---|---|---|---|
| | | | WATERCOLORS: |
| | | | *The Blue Door* |
| | | | *The Road by the Shore* |
| | | | *Follow the Leader* |
| | | | *Sweet Sixteen* |
| | | | *Afterglow* |
| | | | *Path to the Shore* |
| | | | *Sunset* |
| | | | *Fish Houses* |
| | | | *Twin Cedars* |
| | | | *Great Expectations* |
| | | | *Spring Sunshine* |
| | | | *The Cove* |
| | | | *Hauled Out* |
| | | | *Hazy Day* |
| | | | *A Summer Idyll* |
| | | | *Fleeting Clouds* |
| 11/07/–12/12/20 | PAFA | | (10 WATERCOLORS) |
| 2/18/21– | Curtis Library, Brunswick | | *"Cartoon" for War Bonds* |
| 3/15/–4/03/21 | NAD | 91 | *Posing for Her Portrait* |
| 11/19/–12/18/21 | NAD | 29 | *Still Life* |
| 1921 | Chicago | 69 | *A Little Girl in White* |
| | | 70 | *Portrait: My Father* |
| 2/05/–3/26/22 | PAFA | 155 | *A Little Girl in White* |
| 11/17/–12/17/22 | NAD | 157 | *Nude* |
| | | 281 | *A Little Girl in White* |
| 2/04/–3/25/23 | PAFA | 356 | *Nude* |
| 5/30/–6/20/23 | PSA | 16 | *Little Seamstress* |
| 9/13/23 | BCMA | | *Portrait, Professor Woodruff* |

| DATE | LOCATION | CAT. # | TITLE |
|---|---|---|---|
| | | | *Portrait, Manton Copeland, Jr.* |
| | | | *Portrait, Mrs. Thomas Gibson* |
| 11/06/–11/13/23 | Cosmopolitan Club of Bath | | |
| | | | *Mrs. Charles H. McLellan* |
| | | | *President Kenneth C.M. Sills* |
| | | | *Mrs. Charles H. Robinson* |
| | | | *Miss Nelly Baxter* |
| | | | *George F. Noyes* |
| | | | *Jean Terrace* |
| | | | *Mrs. Norman G. Smith* |
| | | | *Manton Copeland, Jr.* |
| | | | *Arthur F. Brown* |
| | | | *Jere Abbott* |
| | | | *Mrs. Thomas Gibson* |
| | | | *W. W. Gilchrist, Sr.* |
| | | | *W. W. Gilchrist, 3rd* |
| | | | *Mending the Flag* |
| | | | *In the Studio* |
| | | | *Her Paris Bonnett* |
| | | | *Coventry Hall* |
| | | | *Sunny Days* |
| | | | *Sketch* |
| | | | *Daydreams* |
| 3/22/–4/20/24 | NAD | 47 | *Reclining Figure* |
| 11/15/–12/07/24 | NAD | 292 | *After Breakfast* |
| 7/02/25 | New England Artists Show–Portland (?) | | *After Breakfast* |
| March 1926 | PSA | | *Portrait, Mrs. Roger Vinton Snow (daughter of Herbert Payson) in riding habit* |

| Date | Location | Cat. # | Title | | Date | Location | Cat. # | Title |
|------|----------|--------|-------|---|------|----------|--------|-------|
| 3/20/–4/11/26 | NAD | 12 | *Corralescean* | | | | | *The Girl in the Riding Habit* |
| | | 29 | *Nude* | | | | | *Portrait of Mrs. Norman G. Smith* |
| 6/01/–12/01/26 | Sesqui-Centennial International Expo in Philadelphia | | | | | | | *A Visit to the Studio* |
| | | | | | | | | *Studio Interior* |
| | | 429 | *Girl in a Riding Habit* | | | | | *The Young Artist* |
| | | 47 | *S. E. Matthews* | | | | | *The French Hat* |
| | | | | | | | | *After Breakfast* |
| 7/12/26– | PSA | | *Deer by Moonlight* | | | | | *Congress Square at Night* |
| | | | *Still Life* | | | | | *Still Life* |
| | | | *Moonlight* | | | | | *A Sunny Corner* |
| | | | *Interior* | | | | | *Fantasy* |
| | | | *Heart of the Woods* | | | | | *Blue and Gold* |
| | | | *Moonlight Marine* | | | | | *Profile* |
| | | | *Portrait, Mrs. Callan* | | | | | *Sunlight and Shadow* |
| | | | *Portrait, Charles H. Payson* | | | | | *The Morning News* |
| | | | *Portrait, Mrs. Payson* | | | | | *The Open Door* |
| | | | *Portrait, Mrs. Roger V. Snow* | | | | | *The Velvet Ribbon* |
| | | | *Portrait, Mrs. C. H. Robinson* | | | | | *The Chimney Corner* |
| | | | | | | | | *Portrait of Arthur F. Brown* |
| | | | | | | | | *Portrait of President Sills* |
| | | | | | | | | *Portrait of Manton Copeland, Jr.* |

POSTHUMOUS EXHIBITIONS

| Date | Location | Cat. # | Title | | Title |
|------|----------|--------|-------|---|-------|
| 5/10/–6/06/27 | Art Alliance of Philadelphia | | | | *Interior, Topsham* |
| | | | | | *Head–Bess* |
| 10/15/–11/05/27 | BCMA | | *Portrait of Alexander Bower* | | *White and Gold* |
| | | | *Portrait of Stephen Mathews* | | *Mending the Flag* |
| | | | *Child in White* | | *Interior (Sketch)* |
| | | | *Portrait of W. W. Gilchrist, Sr.* | | *Watercolors* |
| | | | *Portrait of Philip W. Meserve* | | *The Fishing Sloop* |
| | | | *Portrait of Jean Terrace* | | *Sunset* |
| | | | | | *On the Shore* |
| | | | | | *The Birch Tree* |
| | | | | | *Sand Dunes* |
| | | | | | *Doorway* |

September,
1970            Cosmopolitan Club
                of Philadelphia
                (twenty-five paintings)

06/09/–
    07/28/84    Barridoff Galleries,
                Portland

(Forty-one paintings were exhibited, but only twenty-five
were listed in the catalogue. The names of the others were
lost in a fire.)

*At Her Writing Desk*

*The Gilchrist Family
    at Breakfast*

*Congress Square
    in Winter*

*Girl in Pink*

*Ocean Sunset*

*Forest Path*

*Girl Sewing*

*The Locket*

*Something of
    Interest*

*Daydreams*

*Sun Reflecting on
    the Coast*

*The Liberty Scarf*

*Studio Interior*

*Nelly in the Studio*

*Model Resting*

*Nelly with Her Doll
    Outdoors*

*Parisian Bonnet
    (Portrait of Nelly)*

*Portrait of
    William Wallace
    Gilchrist, Sr.*

*Nelly*

*Bess*

*Portrait of Lucretia,
    the Artist's Wife*

*Nelly and Peggy*

*At Home*

*The Piano*

*Girl in a
    Riding Habit*

11/10/85–
    01/05/86    Woodmere Art
                Museum, Philadelphia

*After Breakfast*

*At Anchor*

*Bed Covering*

*Bess*

*The Birch Tree*

*By the Window*

*Cundy's Point*

*Girl with a Muff*

*A Grandmother*

*Great Expectations*

*The Grey Veil*

*High Tide*

*Interior*

*Kindergarten*

*Landscape*

*The Liberty Scarf*

*Maine Scene*

*Maud (Lady in
    Red Dress)*

*Nelly at Age 5*

*Nelly in the Studio*

*New England Fall*

*The Parisian Bonnet*

*Peggy with Sailboat*

*Portrait of
    Florence Murphy*

*Portrait of W. W.
    Gilchrist, Sr.*

*Portrait of a
    Young Boy–
    Holding Ball*

*Portrait of a
    Young Boy–
    Holding Book*

*Quahog Bay*

*Quahog
    Bay–Swimmers*

*Self Portrait*

*Snow Scene*

*Still Waters*

*Studio Window*

*Sunset*

*Summer Days*

*Two Girls
    on a Bench*

*Uncle John*

*View from Roadside*

*Lucretia always said *Model's Rest* was one of Wallace's better
works. Unfortunately, no one is sure what it looks like. The last
known place it was seen was the Cincinnati Art Museum, which
reports that it was sold in 1945, buyer unknown. It was a small
painting, 10 3/4 x 13 inches.

On March 1, 1917, the American people were outraged to learn that Great Britain had intercepted the now infamous "Zimmerman" note, in which Germany urged Mexico to use the American preoccupation with its imminent entry into World War I to join with Japan in an armed attack on the United States in order to recover territory lost during the Mexican War of 1848. During the month of March, Germany sank five American merchant vessels, giving President Wilson no choice but to ask Congress to declare war. On April 6, the United States entered the war against Germany. By early that summer our forces began to make their numbers felt against the enemy.

*"Cartoon" for War Bonds*

At this time the Gilchrists had been in Maine for two years. Young Bill was in school, and remembered the terror he felt when his class of second graders was told that American boys should be willing to die for freedom if sent to fight in Europe. Bill recalled his father being very much upset by the reports of the war in the *Record*, where graphic accounts were written, often by soldiers returning from the front.

In 1918, as part of his contribution to the war effort, Wallace submitted a unique painting to a national competition for posters used to help sell war bonds. This large piece of work is unlike anything else Wallace ever painted. Some people believe the painting, though ostensibly a vigorous denunciation of the German militarism which he loathed, is also a denunciation of war itself.

Given Wallace's gentle nature, and given his later support of the League of Nations during the controversy that swirled around Wilson's desperate espousal of that doomed institution, this interpretation makes a lot of sense. In fact, Gilchrist felt so strongly that Bill recalls his father becoming involved in a fairly acrimonious dispute with a resident on whether we should or should not join the League of Nations. Because Gilchrist never allowed himself to become embroiled in controversy with neighbors, and because he obviously did not expect to win the competition, we can assume that this painting represents his only "political" statement. Had he lived longer he would be gratified to know that the world now has the United Nations.

*Roses at Mere Point, Brunswick*

## WATERCOLORS

After Gilchrist moved to Maine in 1915, he found outdoor subjects at his doorstep, whereas the area immediately around his home in West Philadelphia offered little he wanted to paint. In the first half of his career, he had less time to paint for pleasure and reputation and concentrated more on portraiture to bring in some money.

In Maine, however, during the years 1919 to 1921, he painted watercolors of outdoor subjects, often including sailboats, people, and tents, to give a feeling of humanity to what otherwise might be simply another landscape. The watercolors included in this book are the best from a selection discovered in the artist's estate and represent a very high level of achievement.

www.meyersphoto.com

*Corner at Roadside*

*Daughters Peggy and Nelly*

*Artist's Wife under Cedars*

*Artist's Daughters Peggy and Nelly*

*Peggy Reading in Rowboat*

www.meyersphoto.com

*Sailing on Quahog Bay, Harpswell, Maine*

*Boats at Bibber's Marina*

*Tide Pool at Giant Steps*

*Looking Over Giant Steps, Bailey Island, Maine*

*Artist's Wife at Hermit Island*

*Looking Past Small Point Harbor*

*Blackwell's Barn*

*Shed at Roadside*

*Cliff on Monhegan*

*Sunset over Peggy Island, Harpswell*

*View from Quahog Landing, Cundy's Harbor*

*Pine Tree at Bald Head*

*Breakers at Giant Steps*

*Cliff by Mere Point*

*Blue Cliffs on Monhegan*

*Rocks off Giant Steps*

*Rugged Cedar on Quahog*

*Brickyard Cove*

*Gilchrist Landing Quahog Bay*

*Rocks by Jaquish Gut*

*Rock at Mill Cove*

*Woods on Catlin Road*

*Clearing the Woods*

*Crib Works to Roadside Dock*

*Sunset on Quahog*

*Sunset on Quahog II*

*Artist's Wife Sitting by Shore at Roadside*

# Index